A BRIDGE IN BABYLON:

STORIES OF A MILITARY CHAPLAIN IN IRAQ

OWEN CHANDLER

chalice
press

Saint Louis, Missouri

ChalicePress.com

Print: 9780820203174
EPUB: 9780827203181
EPDF: 9780827203198

Printed in the United States of America

A BRIDGE IN BABYLON:

STORIES OF A MILITARY CHAPLAIN IN IRAQ

To Emily, Harper, Eleanor, and Sam

At first your love gave me courage.
Then your love sustained me.
Next your love healed me.
And now your love gives me inspiration.
Love matters most.

This book is made possible in part by a generous gift from the Rev. Dr. Gaylord and Diana Hatler in honor and memory of those brave women and men who serve and have served so faithfully as armed forces chaplains.

I wasn't broken, just resting, readying myself for the next big thing.

— David Sedaris

Contents

Introduction:

A Preparatory Message to the Reader

Like most Americans—and you, my readers—I didn't grow up in a military family. I didn't even join until I was thirty-two years old. I know what it is to have no idea what life is like for military men, women, and their families. Like most of you, until my deployment I too had lived my life completely independent of the military, even during the early years of the Iraq war. On the other hand, I deployed to a combat zone at a point in the conflict when most people didn't even know that military operations were still going on. For over a year, my entire universe was dominated by a military engagement that rarely made the news or disrupted the normal rhythm of everyday Americans. During that year of deployment, my family and I lived in the gulf between these worlds—life in the US and life in a combat zone. That is the story of most reservists, those who are no longer really civilians but also not really military, since we are short-time full-timers and I returned to my Reserve unit shortly after the year-long tour.

Shared stories create relationships, and relationships create bridges. When those bridges are crafted in prayer, they become sacred avenues of hope between the unlikely, the courageous, the broken, and the searching.

I intend the stories in the chapters to follow to be a bridge, a way of addressing a common set of dilemmas: the gulfs between the military and civilian worlds, between veterans' complicated experiences and a public that has become accustomed to war, and between the reality of the Guard/Reserve and a perception that only "active duty" military men and women matter. I attempt to create a dialogue between all of these through a story, my story, as a Reserve chaplain deployed to Taji, Iraq, in the US mission against ISIS.

What makes my perspective particularly unique is that I am a minister. I understand my job as crafting a bridge between the sacred stories of our God and the daily stories of my congregation. I am a storyteller of the eternal and true. I forged my stories in prayer and through the eternal story of my Christian faith. My role within the military is chaplain. It is one that is spiritually defined and executed. For those reasons, my memories of Iraq (the biblical Babylon) are inseparable from my theological orientation and capacity to tell a story. In some respects, I lived an elongated psalm reminiscent of the words "By the rivers of Babylon we set and wept when we remembered Zion [home]." It helped that I was stationed by the rivers of Babylon on Camp Taji and that I am a crier!

As a minister of the gospel, story helps me see theological dynamics that are often and easily overlooked. As a soldier and veteran of Iraq, story helps dismantle barriers; story helps to overcome the tendency to say, "You weren't there ... You wouldn't understand," which is exactly how this story begins.

* * *

In 2007, I was basically brand-new to a life in the church. In beautiful Richmond, Kentucky, I learned about ministry and life. Our community was a scenic gateway to the foothills of the Appalachian Mountains. During these days, I made a friend, a marine. He was the son of the senior minister of the church I served as an associate minister. After recently returning from a devastating tour in Iraq, he was making the adjustment to a post-Marine Corps existence. He was unlike any veteran that I had ever met. For starters, he was younger than me. All the veterans I knew were older.

Second, he didn't wear a black baseball-type cap, which I'd assumed was the official uniform of all veterans. These black caps were all basically the same. The brims were typically flat. The crowns were starched and arched. I could see the gold lettering indicating the war, maybe the branch of service too. Sometimes the rank was pinned to one side of the bill. These guys (I don't think that I have ever seen a woman wear one) sat a little taller, a little prouder. Their white tennis shoes were always spotless, and their jeans were unwrinkled. Their presence begged me to make eye contact, especially the Vietnam and Korean War vets. And when I did—because let's face it, those black hats were like tractor beams of patriotic sacrifice—I inevitably nodded my head and thanked them for their service. It had been a conditioned response since September 11, 2001. Deep down, I imagined we all wished that we could engage the veterans in a deeper way, to hear the stories of these men and women, stories of their service, stories of war. I believed it was the task of the American citizen to have some understanding of the sacrifices we asked these military men and women to make on our behalf.

Earlier that year I had had an awkward run-in with an older veteran at a doctor's office. I walked into an overcrowded waiting room where there was a solitary open chair next to an older gentleman wearing a black hat emblazoned with gold lettering that read "WWII Veteran." I felt my anxiety rise as I sat in the open seat. That black hat was the source of my tension. I knew it. It is the same feeling I get when someone has food on their face, but I don't know how to tell them even as I stare uncomfortably at the crumbs. As a minister, I felt like I should talk to him. Clearly, he was proud of his service, but I didn't understand the rules of talking about military service and I didn't want to say something foolish or insensitive. *How do I talk about this man's military service when I haven't a clue what to say or ask?* I thought as I stared at the black hat. And so, I sat inches apart from the man, with no obvious way to bridge the distance between us.

The anxiety I felt next to the black hat was really a longing to connect the gap between the civilian and the military worlds, to make a path between the past and the present, a way to understand the nature of military people's sacrifices.

But that bridge didn't seem to exist in that doctor's office on this day. Instead, I felt only confused and embarrassed.

Like most Americans, I have struggled to understand the threats, the wars, and the scars our veterans have encountered in places like Vietnam or Korea. I didn't even understand the sacrifices our veterans made in the wars in Iraq and Afghanistan. The events of 9/11 seemed like forever ago. It was a complicated reality. Less than 1 percent of the population had volunteered to serve in those recent wars. I didn't have any friends go off to fight in Iraq or Afghanistan. All I knew was that these soldiers and these wars seemed very far away from the waiting room where I was now sitting.

Of course, I was my own worst enemy in situations like this. I created mental movies about each veteran's backstory, which were undoubtedly filled with clichéd misconceptions. For example, I assumed all veterans, especially combat veterans, must have killed someone. I assumed that the Guard and Reserve components were filled with well-connected socialites who were seeking military service without having to become "real" soldiers. I assumed that only "active duty" military personnel were the real soldiers, marines, airmen, and seamen. I assumed that I couldn't understand our veterans' stories because I had not been there.

I carried all these assumptions and stress on my shoulders while in that doctor's office. *What if I say the wrong thing? What if I minimize his service? Worse, what if I trigger a tragic memory?* My mind raced. If all the media reports and common lore were true, then every black hat might as well have "PTSD" stenciled in gold lettering on the back. *He probably doesn't want to talk about his service, anyway,* I told myself and grabbed a convenient magazine.

As I read through the articles, I wondered, *Are civilians supposed to create the bridge?* And then the black hat walked out of the room, but not before I absent-mindedly barked, "America thanks you for your service! We really do!" My pulse slowed again as he walked away. Evidently, I speak on behalf of America now.

Later that year, I made my first attempt at building a bridge with the senior minister's son. I felt a certain obligation to create an avenue by which to cover the distance between us. But how? After fluctuating between trying to play it cool, drinking beer, and thanking him for his service for the hundredth time, I declared failure. What are you supposed to do beyond gratitude? What are you supposed to say next? How do you invite storytelling into the conversation? Obviously I shouldn't ask whether he'd killed anyone. Certainly the topic of sex on deployments was off-limits even if it was a common detail in every war movie I'd ever watched. Presumably I needed to refrain from anything that might have been a scene in Rambo.

One night, after more alcohol than seems possible now, I summoned all the courage from the $5 buckets of beer we were drinking to ask him—to connect with the senior minister's son. I made the leap.

And so, I asked, "What was Iraq like?"

"It was Iraq," he said, in a voice noticeably withdrawn.

So much for a conversation. If I remember correctly, I went and threw up.

Turns out that was an impossible question. It was too broad. It was delivered with judgment, eagerness, and preconceptions. It came off as too familiar, as if we had a shared backstory.

But I never understood any of that until I understood it personally after my own return from service in Iraq.

So, I never broached war again, and he did not volunteer any stories. I let it be.

I doubt that I am the only soul who, after trying to connect with a combat veteran, took failures like this as signs that the world of the warfighter was not meant for the civilian. In the moments following my friend's response, I reverted to meekly thanking him for his service and crossing back over the bridge I had tried to create before it crumbled still further.

It was frustrating. It was defeating. It made me seem callous. Every time I read that another combat veteran had committed suicide, that knowledge reaffirmed to me how fragile the veteran's world must be and how perilous the divide truly was. I wondered whether in the future we would look back at the black hats more as a symbol of pity than pride.

And then my story changed.

I went to Iraq in 2016 with the Army Reserve as a battalion chaplain, part of Operation Inherent Resolve. Though I didn't put on a black hat when I came back from the Middle East, I understood them differently now.

I don't think I was even home a week when I was asked, "So what was Iraq like?"

"It was Iraq." And I looked away, with a mixture of embarrassment and anger.

Like the millions of combat veterans before me, I just didn't know how to answer that overly simplistic question. And honestly, I didn't really want to answer the question. I felt this strong surge of resentment. "You weren't there. You didn't even try to be there. You just let us go, rotation after rotation, and not one thing changed about your life." My mind spiked with pent-up anger even though my lips thankfully stayed shut.

I feared becoming the classic stereotype: a veteran who does not talk about war. I fought these feelings because I didn't really see any reason for them in my situation. I had been lucky in my deployment. I didn't come back with a traumatic brain injury. I didn't come back with PTSD. I didn't have to wash the blood of my brothers or sisters off my uniform. I simply didn't know how to talk about it even though I wanted to share my experience. Of course, some veterans don't ever, ever, ever want to talk about their experiences. There are myriad reasons for their silence, and I respect that right. They earned the right not to say a word. I unequivocally support returning soldiers who wish never to articulate a single thing about those days ever again.

But this wasn't helpful for me. And this wasn't faithful. And so, I prayed. In that season of discernment, God placed a bridge on my heart: Share stories, pray, create relationships, close the divide.

But how?

In some sense, I still don't know the answer to that primary question, but I know the first step involves pushing past basic clichés. Here are some classic examples:

1. *People assume that veterans don't like talking about their experiences because the trauma of war was so intense.* They see the movies. They play the video games. They imagine that war zones are filled with nonstop action sequences where troops are charging through one door after another. For many veterans, this was indeed a significant and scarring part of their reality. But combat

zones can also be super slow. There are significant periods of "hurry up and wait." It often takes hours to make a single move.

Additionally, most soldiers have never even fired their gun in combat, much less killed anyone with it. For sure, those within the combat arms branches of our military, the grunts, the tankers, the cavalry, were asked to do things on behalf of their country that most cannot fathom. They lost friends. They lost parts of themselves externally, internally, and spiritually. They lost their lives.

But for many more, combat experiences were often defined by second-order pressures, battles from sources other than the end of a rifle or the whistle of a rocket. These were the pressures of the POGs (a quasi-derogatory term meaning "persons other than grunts"), the logisticians, the truckers, the doctors, and the mechanics. These military men and women also lost friends or lost their lives. They also lost parts of themselves externally, internally, and spiritually, but they were not the tip of the spear, the first ones in the action.

In the middle of all this chaos were people like me, the chaplain. I nurtured the living, cared for the wounded, and honored the dead. I protected the constitutional rights of free exercise of religion. I existed outside of the chain of command to act as both a barometer of morale and an ethical compass to the command teams. I was a noncombatant. I never carried a weapon at any point during my combat tour. In fact, I have never fired a weapon in uniform. Yet, since returning, I have been asked twice whether I killed anyone in combat, and I clearly disappointed those asking when I said no. "But you got a Bronze Star ..." Their eyes told me everything. To some questioners, the fact that I had never been in the thick of combat diminished my "combat" credibility. Yet, within these wars, even chaplains have lost parts of themselves externally, internally, and spiritually.

2. *People discount reservists as irrelevant.* As a reservist, I was often maligned as not being a "real" soldier. Truthfully, my hardest days in Iraq had nothing to do with ISIS. Instead, my most challenging days involved interactions with the active Army component who frequently looked down on us Reserves. They discounted our professional experiences as irrelevant to being a soldier. They

openly discussed how unintelligent or incapable we must have been not to have been picked to serve on the active side.

Even to get into the war theater as a reservist was a journey of grit, disrespect, and luck. Yet, in order to sustain more than seventeen years of war in Iraq, the Guard and Reserve have been placed in perpetual rotations in combat zones around the world. I doubt the public could comprehend the level of effort it takes to keep a military operation going indefinitely, yet the active component rarely gave us credit for our participation. Indeed, when I was in Iraq, around 60 percent of the American presence was composed of units outside of the active Army, Air Force, and Marines.

My story was familiar to millions of reservist and Guard soldiers, airmen and marines. We weren't famous, well-connected people. We weren't avoiding drafts. If anything, the exact opposite was true. We were mostly working-class or lower-middle-class people who joined to help our country and take advantage of financial incentives like tuition assistance. We shared the experience of being ripped out of our communities and vocations due to events a world away. We did all of this with the prayer that all of our lives would still be there when we got back. We often huddled together to deal with the reality that our lives were seldom the same when we returned. Ours is a story of being inconsequential because we were such a diluted part of the community's population and the public's perception of heroism. Ours is a story of being angry about being deemed inconsequential even though we have helped shape world events. Ours is a story of living with the fact that few people from our cities or towns even know we are gone, and that their lives do not change one bit because of it. How ironic that is, since most Americans are more likely to develop a relationship with a Reserve or Guard soldier than with an active one since most cities are not home to an active post.

3. *People believe that wars are fought exclusively by young men and women.* Most people assume that the most challenging aspect of a combat theater is the enemy. Most of us reservists are old by Army standards. We are in our thirties, forties, even fifties. We have families. The most difficult part of being deployed is missing family. There are holidays and birthdays that we'll never get back. There are parents who have passed without us being able

to say our final goodbyes. There is the fear that our deployment will cause irreparable harm to our children, our marriages, and our relationships. Our deployments are intricately connected to loved ones thousands of miles away.

These clichés are not insurmountable, but they require us, the public, to hear the prayers and stories of our veterans. So, let me share some stories with you.

Before I do, a few final notes: These experiences, these stories, these prayers that I share are not chronological and are often not connected. They are independent, theological memories. All the names and military units' identifiers are omitted to protect the identity and security of those described in these pages. When possible, I obtained the permission of the soldier or contractor to talk about intimate parts of my journey with them. Considering I ministered to over twenty-five hundred personnel who often were in camp one day and gone the next, getting such permission was not always possible.

I will try not to use too many acronyms, and when I do, I will try to include a description of their meaning. Honestly, I didn't always know what I was saying when I was in Iraq. I suspect that I am not the only one. If you say something with enough authority in the military, most people will give you a pass.

Within these pages, I will try to show you what it's like being a Reserve chaplain, husband, and father at war. I think it's easier to share stories from Iraq because of my role. I was not a warrior. I was not a killer. I carried no gun. I shed no blood. For me, war was waged through the stories of those that I counseled.

Ultimately, this is the story of perpetual war, but it is also a story of faith and hope. It is the story of a country engaged in an endless war and an American public that mostly doesn't give that reality a passing thought—as long as those who lose their lives are from other countries because we outsource the fighting to them, and our military does the rest. To the general public, war is costly, but only monetarily. What they know is that the military industrial complex is fed. Jobs are created. Communities, towns, and cities create entire economies that depend on perpetual war, and so everyone turns the other way as a sort of gentleman's agreement, with the wager being a nominal slice of America's sons and daughters. We carry this agreement into our churches, for we rarely discuss or even pray for the wars in which we are still engaged.

Just so you know, I don't wear the black hat. I'm extremely pale and redheaded, so as a rule I rarely wear black. "It washes you out," my grandmother used to say. I also don't wear what has become my generation's version of the black hat—the camo trucker hat with the subdued flag on the front. I call it the combat operators' look. I figure those high-speed guys can wear it if they want. I didn't kick in any doors on my deployment. I don't see any sense in dressing like I did.

Despite it all, well-intentioned souls still ask me, "What was Iraq like?" Even now, several years later, I still don't know how to answer the question, but maybe some of the stories that follow might help bridge a divide I fear is becoming larger and larger every day. Veterans like telling stories, especially if we are allowed to defy your preconceived notions of battle or disappoint your desire to be acquainted with a war hero. I reckon this book of memories is an attempt at that pursuit. The eleven-month-and-ten-day combat tour was one of the most difficult seasons of my life, but it was and continues to be one of the great blessings of my life. I like sharing memories from my time there. I think most of us do. We just need the right bridge.

I pray that these memories will help create bridges between you, the military, the black hats, $5 buckets of beer, and a nation stuck in perpetual war. May they give you insights into the lives of millions of Americans who wear the uniform. Ultimately, may this collection of stories be for you a prayer from Babylon.

Author's Note:

Please Read This

I am comfortable with irony. Kentucky distills it daily. Theology is ripe with it. War perpetuates irony, and I try to capture this in the stories you are about to read.

Since coming home, I have been intrigued (mostly), amused (sometimes), and perplexed (constantly) by people's responses to the profanity of war, specifically around language and sex. For example, consider the following story:

The doctor was tired. His movements were languid. I didn't how he and his staff kept everything clean in the moondust of this distant province in Iraq. As we were talking over the details of the last combat mission of the Iraqis against ISIS, he carried a small stainless bowl over to me. It looked like the kind of cookie tin that arrives at Christmas. I love those butter cookies. They're the perfect metaphor for the holidays: more tissue paper than actual cookie!

Inside the bowl there rattled a mix of twisted metal and small and broken metal mushroom caps. It was a collection of carnage. Each piece had its own story. Each came from the body of a US soldier, or an Iraqi, ISIS combatant, or local bystander—collateral damage. Some of these souls lived, and some died. Their stories on the operating table were all gruesome and gory. The contents of that metal bowl represented some of the worst of what people do to each other. These pieces of shrapnel had come out of men and women and even children.

As I listened to the stories about each of them, my heart ached. As I watched the forlorn eyes of the doctors, I saw pain. In my mind, it was here that I was experiencing the true profanity of war.

But that is the irony ...

In these pages I could recount the most violent and bloody war stories imaginable and you, the reader, would likely permit every detail—every bone crushed, every blood splatter, every brain fragment—to be told without question. Actually, I imagine you would think it would enhance my account. Think about it. These details of war destroy the soul not only of the victim but also of the hearer. Yet, you probably do not consider such details to be profane.

You would be in good company if you thought only of sex and certain kinds of language as being profane. And there's the rub. In this book I have a section on sex, intimacy, and loneliness. I use blunt language and vivid accounts of it all. Undoubtedly, some readers will consider this to be profane and thus inappropriate for a religious audience.

Allow me to suggest that it would be shortsighted to dismiss these details of war. The loneliness, the lack of intimacy, and the destructive sexual habits of military men and women destroy the soul more pervasively and as lastingly as bodily harm. That is the irony of war.

So, I extend grace and an invitation to any of you readers uncomfortable with this specific reality of irony: If you cannot handle conversations on relationships, intimacy, and sexual desire, skip past chapter nine.

Executive Summary

In 2016, an Army Reserve CSSB (combat support and sustainment battalion) out of Phoenix, Arizona, was deployed in support of OIR (Operation Inherent Resolve). This operation was a joint coalition mission of the United States and our global partners to help Iraq defeat ISIS (ISIL or DAESH). The unit was charged with implementing and overseeing part of the ITEF (Iraq Training and Equipping Fund) mission, specifically the equipping and arming of the Iraqi army, sympathetic militias, and Kurdish forces. Their mission was based out of Camp Taji, a far northwestern suburb outside of Baghdad. These soldiers would also create and operate FLEs (forward logistical elements) in the surrounding FOBs (forward operating bases) strategically placed around Iraq for this mission. During the CSSB's time in Iraq, they would be part of the effort to push ISIS from Fallujah, Ramadi, and Mosul.

Chapter 1

The Phone Call: Here We Go!

(Tucson, AZ)

The kitchen was still destroyed. I kept thinking I was nearing a turning point. Surely the effort of the last three days would begin to take shape. I stood back to survey the work. There were no countertops. The cabinets were in disarray. All the appliances were missing except for the refrigerator, which would soon be replaced too. Knowing that the children were in bed, I didn't hide a profanity-laced thought racing through my mind. My watch said 9:30 p.m. It was more than an obvious statement of time. It was also a warning that Thanksgiving dinner was to be prepared in less than thirty-six hours.

The month before, I had almost burned down the house trying to take a shortcut with some brisket and pie. Apparently, the combination of sugar and fat drippings are chemically akin to napalm. Within a minute of my noticing a flame within the oven, the whole stove was on fire. Within an additional minute, the house was so choked with smoke that we struggled to race the children and animals out the door. We were lucky. Between an amazing neighbor and a responsive fire department, there was little damage beyond the oven, hood, and a small portion of the countertop. The damage was localized sufficiently enough that I ruled against making a claim with our insurance. The solution was easy: I would take off the week before Thanksgiving, a time when the church is slow, and repair the kitchen. More than that, I would upgrade the kitchen. Easy.

My beloved, Emily, suppressed a laugh at my clear frustration. She was doing her absolute best to refrain from reminding me of the doubts she'd expressed about the feasibility of the project earlier in the month, especially with such a tight deadline. We made eye contact. As I remember it now, I was in the process of building up the courage to apologize when my cell phone began to ring. It is rarely a good thing when a minister's phone rings after 7 p.m. I began to speculate which church member might be in the hospital. I picked up the phone, and the number ID read the name of one of my favorite lieutenant colonels within my battalion.

"This is Chaplain Chandler."

"Chaplain!" He's a big presence with an even bigger voice.

"Sir! How can I help you this evening?" I asked as professionally as possible with my tired, frustrated voice. I desperately needed to get back to the kitchen. I cavalierly prayed to God that this wasn't another ridiculous drunken soldier situation. I clearly didn't have time to immerse myself in the typical drama of one of our soldiers at this time of night.

"Hey, heads-up. I passed your name on to another LTC. His battalion just got tagged for a push to the Middle East. This is a real deal deployment. They need a chaplain. I told him you were one of the best." I imagined the LTC sitting at a poker table as a group of senior officers played Go Fish with the lives of soldiers as they tried to plug the holes of a roster headed to war.

For the next few moments, I morphed into a clichéd scene from a movie. Everything slowed down. My inner dialogue spun up, which created a muffling effect on all the other noises and voices around me, including the LTC on the phone. I felt the room spin, and though I could see my wife out of the corner of my eye, it felt as if I was all alone.

This LTC and I had a long relationship, and a standing agreement that if he ever learned of a deployment, a real one, where the departing unit needed a solid chaplain, then he had my permission to pass my name onto whomever needed it.

What's a real deployment? you're probably asking yourself. Let me break it down for you.

At the time of this phone call, I served a quartermaster battalion that specialized in fuel management and testing. The unit is tasked with creating the fuel infrastructure for expeditionary campaigns. It makes sense when you think about it. You can't just fill up our military vehicles at the local gas station of the country where you happen to be conducting military operations. The unit follows the first or second wave of military into the war zone and sets up fuel storage and distribution systems and ensures that the fuel is of the appropriate quality. The logistical backdrop of war is surprisingly fascinating.

The fuel infrastructures in Iraq and Afghanistan were already developed by this point and managed by defense contractors. That's the byproduct of years of war. This meant that my battalion was in no danger of ever being deployed unless something new kicked off. Although I found relief in knowing that I was safe from deployment, I also felt guilty about it. Many of my friends had deployed, sometimes multiple times. My family and I had been spared that reality. Chaplains were in short supply, and so the Army, specifically the Army Reserve, pulled chaplains from other units and attached them to deploying units. The term for this was cross-leveling. I figured that if I were ever going to be deployed, it would be by this method.

The US military is engaged in efforts all around the world. The logistics to sustain most of these efforts are immense. The bulk of the military's logistical components are in the Reserves. The result is that the Reserves are perpetually tasked with sending units overseas to support these missions. Not all of these missions required the unit to be placed in a combat zone like Iraq or Afghanistan. In fact, most of them were not in war theaters. They were in places like Kuwait or Qatar.

The LTC and I had agreed that he'd never pass my name on to a mission unless it was going to a combat zone. The reason was simple: I have a wife, children, and a church. If I was going to allow myself to be "volun-told" to deploy, then it needed to be for a weightier assignment, not babysitting young, bored soldiers in a garrison environment where there wouldn't be enough mission to make the sacrifice worthwhile. Besides, only deployments to combat zones are awarded the covetous honor and distinction of the combat patch, a unit insignia that you wear below the American flag on your right sleeve.

In my experience, the combat patch, whether fair or unfair, imagined or real, is what identifies a real soldier. It carries weight, especially in the Army Reserve. It also connects, as soldiers create bonds over experiences in Iraq or Afghanistan. Soldiers automatically give one another a degree of respect when they see that on a sleeve. And they look. It is the second thing soldiers look for after identifying the other's rank.

Those who don't have a combat patch are referred to as "slick-sleeves." This is not a term of endearment. These soldiers are clearly part of the outgroup. They are perceived as naïve or green. If you happen to be an older officer or enlisted, then other soldiers assume you've dodged deployments if you're a slick-sleeve. Fundamentally, a slick-sleeve has to earn respect, to prove their knowledge and professionalism. It's not a deal breaker to be without a combat patch, but it does mean you have to work harder.

I was a slick-sleeve.

"What do you think, Chaplain?" His question brought me back into the moment.

"Of course, sir. I'll be good to go." The words just hung there. I must have been out of my mind.

By this point, Emily knew this was a different type of conversation. Her brows furrowed. She kept shifting from one foot to the other. She was doing this thing where I could tell she was trying to read my body language. Her intentional eye contact was unsuccessful in gaining access to my mind. She was concerned—that much was evident. There was nothing I could do at this point, so I sought to avert my eyes. I felt like an ass.

The LTC boomed, "Perfect! Within the hour, the unit's BC is going to call you."

"Roger that, sir." And the phone went silent.

I turned to Emily. There were already tears in her eyes. Clearly, she had assumed the worst. I think that's common in situations like this. I exhaled. This was one of the few times her assumption was on target.

"I'm being deployed." And just like that our world turned upside down.

Without thinking, I covered the distance to embrace her. We stood holding each other—I can't remember for how long. Her head was buried in my chest. My chin rested on the crown of her head. There wasn't a breath of space between us. I held tight because I was at a loss for what I should say next. I imagined Emily felt the same. Her grip wasn't loosening either.

I tried to give us some grace within this moment, but I was anxious. I felt as if I should have known the perfect thing to say at this moment. In the movies, the soldier preparing to leave always has that perfect line, but I didn't. I mean, how do you prepare for this situation? Though we had always known this exact moment might happen, after four years in the Reserve, it felt improbable.

In reality, I never thought it would go down like this. I'd assumed that deployments came with more of a warning. There was an ARFORGEN (army force generation) cycle in the Army Reserve that projected out several years the deployability of a given unit. The cycle was composed of a several-year training window followed by a deployment, followed by a reset time period before a move back into training. I had always imagined there would be a discussion among the command staff centered on whether or not the unit would deploy the upcoming fiscal year depending on where the unit was in that cycle. The last thirty minutes shattered all of these assumptions.

I could feel Emily sobbing quietly. I felt my own tears fall. We continued to hold tight.

"I'm scared," she whispered.

"I know. Me too," I whispered back.

I didn't have any details other than the one that had just turned our life completely upside down.

"What do you know?" I could feel her move to look up.

"Not much," I honestly replied. "The call was LTC U. He just finished a meeting with a bunch of colonels. They were tasked with filling a roster for a deployment to what looks like Iraq. They needed a chaplain, and my name was given. Just like that."

"Can you say no?" Her voice was regaining its strength.

I thought about obscuring the truth on this question. I didn't know how she would respond if I told her that I had allowed LTC U to volunteer me. But I couldn't hide the truth from her. I figured that she needed to be able to trust everything I said about this deployment from here on out. I didn't want her second-guessing the information I relayed to her during our time apart.

"I probably could have turned it down, but it wouldn't be good." I said it as matter-of-factly as possible. "I haven't been. It's my turn. It wouldn't be fair if they pulled another chaplain who's already been over there."

The tears returned; so did the sobs. I felt as if I'd broken something in her. It was horrible, and the silence of the next several minutes did not relieve any of the tension.

"Do you know when you are leaving?" Her head lifted again.

"Not really, but I think it's within the next five or six months. I get the sense they are trying to get out the door as soon as possible. There is another colonel who is supposed to call me tonight with more details."

"Do you have to answer the phone?!"

I chuckled, and then I immediately felt guilty for doing so.

Right as the words were beginning to form in my mouth, our infant woke up. Emily rushed off to nurse him back to sleep. I stood there for a while, uncertain what to do. Eventually I grabbed a wrench and looked at the kitchen. For the next thirty minutes, I must have tightened the same bolt without even really knowing what I was doing. When the phone rang, it startled me.

"This is Chaplain Chandler," I tried to say with a deeper voice than was normal.

"Chaplain, I'm LTC G." His words were quick, but strong.

"Yes, sir," I reported back. Anxious, I thought about making a joke about being invited to an upcoming camping trip, but I thought better of it.

After an awkward bit of silence he said, "I am the battalion commander of a unit tasked to deploy downrange. I need a chaplain. I understand that you are good and available. You got time to talk?"

"Of course, sir." I was apparently incapable of articulating much beyond just saying the word *sir* a lot.

For the next ten minutes, I mostly listened. His voice was familiar and calming. It seemed as if he knew what he was doing and what he was saying. This was great because I didn't really know what to say or ask. I tried to maintain a professional bearing even as my mind struggled to keep pace with the conversation.

By the end of those ten minutes, I had learned two things that surged an already adrenaline-filled mind. First, this deployment was to beef up the effort against ISIS. The implicit takeaway on this front was that we would be directed to deploy to Iraq though he could not officially say so. Second, the whole unit would need to be out the door and headed toward the theater within three months rather than the standard six-months-to-a-year timeline. I would need to wrap up my family life and professional matters within a month or two at the latest in order to be ready for an intense one-month train-up exercise in Phoenix. That one month would be crucial to make the transition to the official pre-deployment training in Fort Hood, Texas.

First impressions were important. I prayed that I sounded coherent and capable, but I doubted that I did much beyond not setting off any red flags. For his part, LTC G was articulate, insightful, and sensitive about the burden he was tasked to execute. I was impressed. He was deliberate about learning the depth of my experience and the value I could bring to this deployment. It was apparent that he valued the role of the chaplain even as he honestly conveyed that he held no religious convictions himself. In my mind and in my heart, I felt God's reassurance.

"So, if there aren't any other questions, I just need to know your status. I know it's late. I think I understood that you have a family with little ones, so if you need to think it over some more, feel free. Just get back to me soon. Okay?" His tone was empathetic.

I thought for a moment. I felt peace.

"Sir, I'm good. I'll be ready."

"All right. Here we go!" And then the phone went silent.

* * *

I looked up from the kitchen. Emily was not back yet from nursing the baby to sleep. I was unsure whether I should peek into the room. I looked at the cabinets. They were all still in limbo. There was no sense pretending that I was going to accomplish anything else tonight. I placed the wrench on the floor, letting go of all the things that still needed to be done. I would make sure it got done before Thanksgiving. I looked at my watch and it showed 11 p.m. The birth of my three children had taught me that life can change dramatically within a few moments. With each first cry, my future story had changed. I felt that same sensation now. The future would be different, but I still felt peace. The presence of the Holy was here.

I crept into my daughters' room. At ages five and three, they preferred to sleep together even though each had her own bed. I curled up with them. I listened to them breathe. I felt their warmth. I spent those moments imagining what dreams must be delighting their little souls. I couldn't believe that I would spend most of the following year away from them. I prayed that the same peace which centered me now would wrap around them in the morning.

During this time of prayer, my mind drifted to a new place. I found myself wondering about the other soldiers receiving phone calls tonight. To be sure, my family wasn't the only one to have their holiday week turned upside down. I later learned that around five other soldiers with specialty MOSs (military occupational specialty codes, i.e. the Army name for your position) got phone calls. In my mind, I saw men and women in tears. I saw them scared. I saw them frustrated. There were clouds gathering over their houses. There was uncertainty. I prayed for God's peace to be with them as well.

At some point, I felt the hall light creep across my face, and I knew that Emily was searching for me. I gave the girls another kiss and crawled back out of bed, avoiding the kitchen, and went into the bedroom where Emily was resting in her rocking chair next to the bed. She was so beautiful under the serene, soft light of an old lamp. I moved across our bedroom. She didn't look up or hear me as she was so lost in thought.

I looked down at her. "The other unit's LTC called."

The tears returned to both our faces. I could instantly tell that she had prayed that the last two hours had been a dream. I can't remember the last time we cried so much. Wrapping my arms around her again, we swayed to the beats of our hearts.

"It's Iraq. I'll need to be ready to leave within the next month or so because of some additional training. I'm sorry." I let the last words trail off.

"I don't know how not to be afraid right now," she said.

"I don't either. I keep thinking that there will be a swell of courage or something, but I can't find it. I do sense a peace about this, for what it's worth. I'll be okay. You and the kids will be okay too," I replied. I wasn't lying.

We stood holding each other. I wondered how many spouses have stood in this same position over the last fifteen years as they contemplated the same impending reality. I wondered how many of my friends and neighbors would ever know or understand the emotions we were steeped in right now. I felt something push me back into the present, back into her arms, back into her heart. I took this cue from the spirit and I prayed the first of many deployment-specific prayers. I prayed that she felt the same peace I did.

Part of me wondered whether we were going to let the night dance by without another word, but she pulled back and looked at me with tear-stained eyes. "You are still going to finish the kitchen before Thanksgiving, right?"

We laughed. And we cried more. And then sleep finally overtook us.

Chapter 2

The Battle Cry: Victory or Valhalla

(Phoenix, AZ, to Fort Hood, TX, to Kuwait to Iraq)

"It's got to inspire fear." A Spartan stoicism formed each word.

The company commander repeated the thought to the soldiers surrounding him. He was pacing within the battered makeshift TOC, or tactical operations center. Was he being serious, or was this sloganeering a ruse?

"This is what we will use to motivate us after every formation as we prepare for battle," he added.

The captain was a well-intentioned leader, seasoned from years on active duty with multiple deployments to his credit. Yet, I questioned his motivation techniques. In a previous troop accountability formation back in Phoenix, he had revealed that at least one soldier under his leadership had died in each of his deployments. I remember being stunned.

"Kill! Kill! Kill!" Screeched one of the soldiers in the room.

I snorted. Surely this conversation couldn't be serious.

We were finally nearing the end of deployment training in North Fort Hood. This left us with a considerable amount of unaccustomed downtime. I am sure it was supposed to be a blessing, a chance to catch up on laundry, maybe even get some sleep. For me, it was just too much time for my overactive mind to fashion scenarios of my doom. So, I wandered around the confined post looking for diversion.

"No. Let's be more creative," the leader resumed, as if this should have been obvious from the beginning.

I sat a short distance off to the side with a notebook in hand. This conversation had been driving along like this for the last forty-five minutes and I was determined not to miss it. The captain was eager. The collection of soldiers matched his intensity with an aggressive earnestness.

I smirked. "Shouldn't our motto be more suited to what we actually do?"

Their wounded pride stared back at me.

"I mean ... we handle logistics ... on C-130s and Chinooks and local contracted truckers ... at night ... We are like UPS but with weapons qualifications and secret clearances."

I don't think I was winning any points.

"Anyways ..." one of the sergeants responded.

Eyes rolled and refocused on the task at hand. If I could've read their thoughts, I was pretty sure they weren't seeing me in a particularly positive light. I mean, what did I know? I was just the chaplain. I wouldn't be carrying any weapons. I would have a personal security detail. I wouldn't be asked to do any real soldiering.

Evidently, logos and slogans were a vital preparation for the warfighter, especially to the reserve combatant. At least, that's what I was learning. Or at least, that's what we were determined to spend most of the last few days of our training discussing. I got the sense that we were trying to compensate for a perceived lack of lethality that the active Army trainers were implying about us. That theme of proving our worth as reservists would be a persistent one throughout our deployment.

"I've got a good one!" The senior noncommissioned officer sat straight up.

"Well?" a voice asked. The room was his.

"What if we did something like ... 'Victory or Valhalla!'" He let the resounding words echo among the hearts of his soldiers. From the tone of his voice, one would have thought that he was conjuring the power of the Ark of the Covenant.

The room was heavy with silence. I felt bad for the NCO. I read the stillness as an indictment against his suggestion. Slowly, however, one nodding head turned into two nodding heads, and before long the room in agreement.

"That's it!" declared the first sergeant definitively.

I sat incredulous.

"Y'all. How in the holy hell does 'Victory or Valhalla' even remotely make sense?" Blank stares. This was absurd. "Can't we just shout something like 'Deliverers of Destruction' or 'Carriers of Chaos'?" I was trying to not laugh because this was obviously important to them.

The conversation was over. Their faces said that they were now ready for war. I fell silent.

In my mind, I wondered whether the biblical warriors of old and their leaders used similar rhetorical tools as motivation. I imagined David preparing to stand before Goliath as those around him shouted, "Sling of Salvation!" I wondered if Moses stood before the parted waters and cried out to the Israelites as Pharaoh's chariots chased them, "Plagues and Pestilences!" I finished with this note to myself:

I should probably start realizing that these young men and women may be asked to do things that I won't have to do ... like kill. Victory or Valhalla it is.

* * *

And so, I guess we were ready. All the other soldiers seemed prepared. We looked the part in our new uniforms and gear. Like children on the first day of school, we swaggered and conversed with unearned confidence. With the company motto in place, we set our sights upon our nation's enemies.

But there was a problem: As a reservist, it took forever to head to a combat zone.

Since this was a new experience for me, I was woefully naïve about the process required for insertion into a war theater. In the movies, the arrival at the destination is always depicted in an intense way. There's the drama of a blackboard with a clearly defined mission and specific objectives. There are close-up shots of steely eyes searching enemy positions on the horizon. There are backstory flashbacks to training and moments of personal perseverance. And always there are tearful families waving flags and children dancing between the legs of adults as their loved ones march toward glory and history.

As a reservist, only one of these would be true for me: my son playing at the feet of my weeping wife and sobbing daughters. I could hear their cries even as I turned the corner out of their sight. Agonizingly, my family and I went through this twice more when the Army repeatedly and unexpectedly sent us back to Phoenix, Arizona. One of the last times, Emily and I couldn't bear putting the children through another goodbye. Instead, as my family slept, I walked outside in downtown Phoenix at 2:30 a.m. under a drizzly, darkened sky and hailed a cab to the airport.

A couple of years later, I would sit at a Veterans Day breakfast listening to stories of Vietnam vets. I told them that I didn't know how they had done it back then. Their tours were devastating, deadly, and long. They shook their heads. They told me that they didn't know how I had done it. As teenagers, they hadn't had to leave their small children behind when they left.

The final departure carried a heavy emotional tone. As our unit boarded a plane back to Fort Hood, absent were the darkened humor, talk of mission, and normal small talk. The mood was quiet. Eyes were tearstained.

The last two months between Arizona and Texas had been a series of fits and starts, hurry up and wait, move, move, move, hold fast, stand down. We had arrived at Phoenix under the clear impression we were heading straight to Iraq. It focused us. There were endless horse blanket to-do lists that, once finished, led only to another round of required training, medical screenings, or mission briefings. There were fights with our higher echelon units over when we got paid and where we were allowed to stay during the training. We were often moved from hotel to hotel depending on budget constraints. Twice we were told that the mission probably wouldn't happen, and soldiers were asked to see if they could get their jobs back. Inevitably, the mission would come back online, and those same soldiers would be asked to leave their positions again. Some of the veterans of previous deployments revealed that deploying on the active duty side was much cleaner and more streamlined. Anything had to be better than what we were living.

When we left Buckeye, Texas, for Fort Hood, we also left with a change of mission. It deflated us. We were now tasked with a mission to Kuwait. This would now be the focus of our pre-deployment training in Texas. A new list emerged at the mobilization site, and depressingly, many of the items were the same ones we'd just finished in Arizona. Once these basic items were completed again under the official eyes of the active Army trainers, there was enhanced training slated specific to our positions and the mission.

In Texas, we met every challenge placed before us even as our team changed due to medical disqualifications and additional cross-leveled soldiers. Some of the medical disqualifications were regrettable and life changing. One soldier learned of a surprising and rare condition that not only ended the soldier's deployment but also their military career. For soldiers like this, pre-deployment training felt more like a body blow than a sharpening.

In the beginning, there was this rush of adrenaline as you prepared your mind for the possibility of what awaited. It was exhausting, especially for the first timers like me. I woke up each day steadying myself for the journey to Iraq, and then I made the mental switch to Kuwait. After a while of circling the same training point over and over again in the sterile environment of North Fort Hood, it almost seemed surreal. I got to the point that I forgot that we were actually going to deploy.

But then we did.

A few days after the motivational slogan of a lifetime and after one month in North Fort Hood, we stood in an empty airplane hangar. The space was vast. It swallowed the mood. I imagined that in the heyday of the wars the commanders stood thousands of soldiers within these walls. The hangar was centered on a set of storefront doors leading to the special tarmac, a gateway to our mission.

We sat for hours waiting in that hall. There were bleachers, but apparently it wasn't worth the installation time to pull them out for us since we were only around forty in number. So, we collapsed on bags nervously packed, and waited. We stared at our phones. We tried not to think.

And then the order was given: "FORM UP!"

I watched as the unit assembled. I noticed the faces. They were expressionless for the most part. I scanned the formation and noticed the ones that were missing from those first days from Buckeye. In their place, there were now soldiers from California, Missouri, South Dakota, and elsewhere. Their faces betrayed nothing, but I was sure my anxiety was written all over my face. This was it. We were finally going.

"Company!"

"Platoon!"

"Attention!"

The instructions were barked out. Hard times—a military term for a nonnegotiable time—were given. Warnings were stated. Ubiquitous mentions of battle buddies filled in all the spaces in between. There were no final words of wisdom to help us frame this experience. Nothing. When it was all done, the command pattern repeated itself, but this time, the formation shouted, "Victory or Valhalla!"

I wish that I could say it sounded proud and powerful, but it didn't. It was as stupid I thought it would be.

We boarded the plane for Kuwait. In my journal I wrote these words:

We walked out of an empty terminal. The sun greeted us. On this secluded tarmac, three large planes waited. The one with an honor guard welcomed us to our plane. The walk to the plane was straight out of a movie. We were single file and the pace was introspective. Tears filled my eyes and I fought them back. I was not ready to cry for this. We were treated like heroes, but it feels so premature. I sense that we are poised to earn their esteem. One soldier pulled me aside. He asked for prayer. I prayed for him and the beautiful family that I saw him with a few days ago. As the plane started to taxi, I sent Emily one last text, 'and so I am off...' and then I shut my phone down.

The plane ride was almost uneventful as we made our way to Ramstein, Germany, the first stop before we landed in Kuwait. Then the Army threw us a new curveball. Somewhere over the Atlantic, our mission changed. Kuwait would not be our final stop after all. The months of preparation for a logistics mission involving boats and ports were gone. We had a new country. We had a new mission. We were heading to Iraq.

In light of those developments, landing in Kuwait was as anticlimactic as it was disorienting. Most of us had not slept in two days. Moods were foul. Hygiene was lacking. As we exited the airplane, the air was putrid and salt-laced. It reminded me of Panama City Beach in Florida. I laughed as we boarded charter buses. The sun was still an hour away from rising.

The Army sent us to Camp Beuhring for the short term. I didn't give it much thought. We would later learn that there were discussions happening at echelons far above us about whether we could handle the Iraq mission. As we neared the front gates, the sun offered enough light to take in the surroundings. I scanned the landscape. There were camels everywhere. I smiled. I felt punchy.

We unloaded the bus and formed up. I tried to listen to all the instructions, but I was exhausted. A few people shouted, "Victory or Valhalla," and I embarrassingly knew the formation was over. I peeled off to use the restroom, but there were only long rows of Porta-Potties. Stepping into one, I was assaulted by the smell of mothballs. *What?* Apparently, the Kuwaiti nationals contracted to be custodians of the Porta-Potties used the mothballs because they thought the item was a panacea that disinfects and freshens—cheaply.

Several days later, we were still waiting for the final authorization to move to Iraq. Emily had emailed me asking what Kuwait was like. I could tell from her tone that she was concerned. I imagined many of the novice deployers' families were similarly anxious. Sitting in a comfortable Internet café, I quickly wrote back to her:

Emily,

Camp Beuhring is something. How to capture it for you? You know how in the beginning of a war movie there is always a scene where the helicopter flies in bringing the protagonist's team? Think of Forest Gump. Remember how they land and look around to see one huge party happening? There are cookouts and music and laughing. Somewhere in the distance there is an omnipresent volleyball game playing. Can you picture that? Okay. That's what Camp Beurhing is like except there are camels and sandstorms instead of jungles and snakes. I am safe. We are all safe. BTW: Our mission changed back to the original. More later.

Victory or Valhalla. Gasp. Vomit.

But we were stuck in Kuwait.

I woke up each morning with the same shot of adrenaline that I'd had back in Phoenix Like the months leading to this point, nothing was easy. Our mission almost changed again. There was an active Army unit jockeying to replace us for the mission. Each day began the same way:

"Form up."

We waited for news of the movement. We were ready for Iraq, but there was no new news.

Instead, standard instructions were barked out. Hard times given. Warnings shared. Ubiquitous mentions of battle buddies filled in all the spaces in between.

"Company!"

"Platoon!"

"Attention!

"Victory or Valhalla!"

"Fall out."

And then the day ended without any change.

By the end of two weeks, the adrenaline was gone. So too was the unit's enthusiasm to shout our company motto. Many suspected that the delay was due to an impending change of mission. Among all the uncertainty, the leaders kept us forming up though. I could almost see the panic in the captain's eyes as he sensed our diminishing motivation.

* * *

There were definite benefits to being held up in Kuwait. For starters, I was able to drink coffee at the Starbucks on post every morning. Since there was Wi-Fi there, I video chatted with the family regularly. Also, the food within the DFAC (the cafeteria) was great, and there was tons of it. Luckily, there were several gyms scattered all over the installation, including a CrossFit box, so I didn't gain any weight.

In Kuwait, I made a friend: Chief. It was a development that shaped the rest of my deployment. He was a very senior-ranking chief warrant officer. He was on leave during the Phoenix days, and since he ran the maintenance shop, our training in Fort Hood didn't overlap. To be honest, Chief was intimidating. He had a no-nonsense demeanor and a mustache. Very few people in the military were able to pull off a mustache, but Chief did. Most soldiers, enlisted and officers alike, treated him with reverence.

Back home, I had struggled with making friends as an adult. Yet, one day, after the unit's morning ritual and ebbing shouts of "Victory or Valhalla," I made rounds among the temporary offices. I liked to walk into a room and see if I could stir up conversation, maybe create some good-hearted mischief. I got to talking to the maintenance NCOs, and before long, Chief looked over my way with an almost grin. It took a lot to get a mustached soldier to smile, so I figured I must have been extra funny that day.

"You play ping-pong, chaplain?" he called out in his West Virginian accent.

"Chief, if you can find it in a church basement or a redneck's backyard, I can play it," I responded. The room chuckled.

"I'm heading up to the MWR [Morale, Welfare, and Recreation center] later. You want to play?"

"I don't know, Chief. This isn't one of those scenes in the war movie where the rookie gets hustled, is it?" We both laughed.

Later that night, we played ping-pong. The next night we threw darts. Later that week we organized volleyball games. By the weekend, we had put together a cookout with a cornhole tournament. By the following week, I had found a truly great friend, which was a blessing because each morning started the same way in that dusty hellhole.

"Form up."

The instructions were barked out. Hard times given. Warnings shared. Ubiquitous mentions of battle buddies filled in all the spaces in between.

"Company!"

"Platoon!"

"Attention!

"Victory or Valhalla!"

"Fall out."

At least now I had a battle buddy.

* * *

Sometime in the second week of Camp Buehring, small segments of our unit were pushed into Iraq under the cover of darkness. It started with the sections required to set up the headquarters. Then the leaders from the sections covering operations. At the morning formations, fewer and fewer people were forming the ranks and bellowing out the company battle cry.

Every day I checked in on the secret phone line with the battalion commander whether this was the day that I would get to push north. The answer was always no. I was living a déjà vu moment. Like in Fort Hood, I was circling the same point over and over again in Kuwait. It seemed almost surreal. It got to the point that I forgot that we were actually going to complete a mission in Iraq.

But then we did. Or at least I did.

On Friday the thirteenth, I went to the phone bank at the USO. I needed to place a call. I did not have to wait long for a spot. I called home. Emily answered. In the background I could hear a family friend. I'd forgotten she had a margarita lunch planned.

"It will be a few days before you hear from me again. I love you, Emily. I have to go."

She knew what that meant. I could hear muffled tears.

"I love you, Owen."

And then we hung up.

I gathered all my bags. I had packed and repacked these same bags eight times in the last three months. I hollered at Chief. He indicated that he would be up several days later as part of the next push. I held a short meeting with my chaplain assistant, the individual tasked with my security. To his disappointment and confusion, I told him that he would not be coming with me on this flight. There were not enough seats on the transport.

"Hold fast. You'll be up in a few days."

"Sir, you are seriously saying that you are flying into Iraq tonight without me? Without any security?"

"Yep. Don't tell my wife. I'll be good to go. See you soon." And then I walked off.

The sky turned to dusk as I hopped into the truck heading for an Air Force hangar. I was dressed in all my Kevlar. I strapped on my helmet and walked into the terminal. Eventually my name was called, and I headed to the flight line.

Crouched in the belly of a darkened C-130, I crossed into Iraq. I shared the experience with a cargo hold full of supplies and a smattering of soldiers and contractors. A few hours after take-off, the plane began to corkscrew over northern Baghdad as we prepared to land. Some of the old-timers had prepped me for the combat landing, but this was unlike any rollercoaster that I had ever ridden. I felt a surge of adrenaline that I didn't even think was possible.

The wheels hit the runway. It was jarring. Even securely buckled, I felt like I was falling from my seat. I looked around at the other soldiers. They were securing their gear and checking their weapons, which had been loaded prior to takeoff. I had been told that I was the only one getting off at this stop.

"When the cargo hold opens, move carefully and quickly straight out. Do this so that you don't get burned by the jets. Once you are out, take a hard right. There will be someone there to guide you to safety." The NCO was clear, concise, and concrete.

Honestly, I felt fear. I lamented not waiting for my chaplain assistant. The hatch opened. I gathered my stuff and I marched. I felt the heat of the jets, but I did as I was told and stayed in the middle. In my mind, I wondered how vulnerable I was to attack at this very moment. I imagined shots ringing out around my position as I ducked into safety. I closed my eyes and prayed.

Somewhere from my right, I heard a voice yelling, "Chaplain!"

I made the hard right and hustled to the source of the voice, but there was not much light in the area. I was as close to running as I could muster with all the weight I was carrying. I locked on to the direction of the voice again. I hoped for the sake of my safety that the bellowing soldier had a really big gun.

I felt a hand reach onto my shoulder. I jumped and turned. I stopped and I did a double take.

In front of me, there stood an older gentleman, probably in his late fifties, wearing khaki pants, a plaid shirt, New Balance white shoes, a hard hat, and a safety reflector vest. He looked like someone doing construction outside of my church in Tucson.

"Welcome to Taji!" he shouted. There was no machine gun. There wasn't an armored transport. There was just a guy who looked like he'd bought his "uniform" from JCPenney. Iraq would be more different than I could ever imagine.

Confused, I saluted. "Victory or Valhalla?"

Chapter 3

The Chaplain's Day: Twenty-Four Seven

Iraq was hot. It was unbelievable. The sweat never stopped. I never truly acclimated to it. It created this perpetual film of dirt, sunscreen, and perspiration, which left a residue on every surface I touched. There was no break from the heat. The humidity from the river kept the hot air trapped. Even in the middle of the night, I dripped beads of moisture. The Army tried to ease the situation a bit. In each CHU, or containerized housing unit, there was a small window unit. Our little air conditioner, like most of the AC units in all of Iraq, had not been able to keep up lately. Technology can only do so much when it is 120 degrees outside. I even considered sleeping in my office a few nights because the AC was cooler there for some reason.

One night, I woke up in a kiddie pool of sweat. It was the second time I had awakened to use the restroom. As I peeled myself off the bed, I chuckled at all this perspiration, because in my mind it made the nightly frequent trips to the bathroom seem absurd. How did I even have fluid left in my bladder right now?

Muscle memory was a blessing. I could make the fifty-yard walk to the latrine in my shower shoes while dodging rocks and concrete barriers with one eye fully closed and the other barely open. I wouldn't even say I had to wake up fully anymore, which was perfect, because it was easier to fall back asleep. As I walked past the rows of CHUs, I cursed all the nineteen- and twenty-year-olds. They had no idea how fortunate they were to be able to sleep through the whole night. The old man curse would hit them one day too. These were the thoughts running through my mind as I made my way to the facility.

As a point of orientation on the FOB, the restrooms and showers were located in a converted single-wide trailer outside of the protected CHUs. There were three large silos on the outside that housed the grey wastewater, the potable water, and the sewage. There were huge signs warning people to refrain from drinking, touching, or even thinking about the sewage. In the military world, when I saw that level of signage, I could bet it meant that someone had done one of these things. As I walked, I prayed the same prayer I did most nights: I pleaded with God that I might find favor and that my favorite stall would be available. Between the stickiness and the artwork, most of the stalls were disgusting. I preferred the one where the troop graffiti wasn't as graphic. This time of night, I didn't need any reminders about all the sex I wasn't having; nor did I need to lament our soldiers' inability to understand basic rules of grammar.

As I finally neared the door to the latrine, my mind processed the pending deep satisfaction of a promised relief. I opened the door. Wading through the thickened heat of the shower steam and bodily fluids, I made the turn to the last stall on the right. And then I heard it:

"Hey! Chaplain!"

I knew the husky voice, but my mind was still sleeping. Looking at my watch, it was barely after 0200. Damn. I just needed to pee. I pried my eye open a bit more to see the familiar face of a sergeant from another task force. He was a good dude, but he was way too awake for me. I acted out a comical salute and kept my path true. I couldn't stop. I wouldn't stop.

"I was just thinking that I wanted to run into you, but I got switched to nights. I just stopped by here before I picked up my lunch at the DFAC. You busy?"

I slowed my march a bit. I put on my best attempt at a sincere smile as I continued to pace toward the last stall. "Of course I'll make room for you. You still got my number? I'll rearrange my schedule. Give me a call and we'll figure out the time." Boom! Situation handled.

The pressure on my bladder threatened to fully wake up my other eye. As I strode past him, he said in a lowered voice, "Roger, that sir." I looked back.

Even with only one eye open, I could see that this guy was hurting. His eyes were red. He was about to cry. The moisture on his face wasn't sweat. On this deployment, I learned that there was something about the latrine that freed a man's vulnerability. I had shed a few tears in these stalls myself. His pain moved me—reluctantly, but it moved me.

And so, I stopped beside him. He needed me.

It was just so late. I wanted to sleep, but this was my job. Unlike most of the personnel on Taji, the role of a chaplain never stopped. It was always there. In fact, I felt as if I was called on more often in the in-between moments of the day and the after-hours blocks at night than any other time. Incredulously, I heard the words leave my mouth: "We can talk about it now, if you like."

How did I even get to where this was normal?

I thought about that question as we sat down. I had come a long way from the discombobulation of my first night in country. Deploying to a combat zone was intense, especially your first time, especially the first few nights. Waking up as a stranger in a strange land's war disoriented the soul. In a battle such as this, the unfamiliar darkness was compounded by an unseen enemy outside of concrete T-walls less than a mile from your bed. It was an uneasy sensation. This was not an abstract scenario. This was not one of the many training exercises reservists endure in the lead-up to departure. This was the real deal; elements of the enemy—ISIS, in our case— inhabited the neighborhoods surrounding our position. Their goal was simple: Kill as many of us as possible. They were opportunistic killers. They relied on our mistakes, our complacency, and luck. I had come face-to-face with this disorientation the moment my C-130 touched ground after corkscrewing from the sky. I had grabbed my gear and headed into a darkened unknown.

I had arrived in Taji, Iraq, on Friday the thirteenth. No joke. I prayed this was not an omen of things to come. My first day there did not help with this uneasiness. We were welcomed with the distinct sounds of the IDF (indirect fire) sirens indicating mortars. That same evening was filled with episodic spurts of gunfire from unknown locations. This place manipulated my deepest fears.

As a minister of the gospel and one who had seen the face of death so often in the faces of my parishioners, I told myself that I was not a fear-filled soul. I recited passages of scripture from Matthew like "Do not be afraid of those who can kill the body but cannot kill the soul." The disorientation of Iraq opened the door for a voice I had never heard before. It was dark. It was powerful. In the silence of that first night, this troubling voice whispered, "You will never see your children again; they will have no memory of you; and another man will take your place." It was the most terrified I have ever been.

For those who had deployed before, this sensation of disorientation was nothing new. "You drive on," they said. If those guys were nervous, they revealed nothing. I didn't know how they did it. For those of us who were on our first tour into a combat theater, our first few nights in Iraq were restless, to say the least. I startled at every creak and noise. I slept maybe a couple of hours each night that first week. I was certain that each sound was the call of death. My mind tormented me with mini-movies playing scenes of all the ways I was going to be brutally killed. The whole thing seemed so absurd and dramatic now, yet at the same time—at least for me—it was all-encompassing and inescapable.

And the disorientation was completely absurd. Prime example: Restlessness and forced hydration didn't mix well. It didn't matter how much I sweat. My biology repeatedly betrayed me early in the deployment as I struggled to ignore the pressure in my bladder to make the zero-dark-thirty trip to the latrine. During the first nights in Iraq, the fifty-yard, late-night trip to the restroom was terrifying. I would curse myself. *If I die because I drank too much water, that's going to be beyond embarrassing.* I'd walk to the latrine on these nights completely wired with adrenaline, always looking for where there were bunkers or places I could take cover if the sirens went off. It wasn't easy to fall back to sleep after these trips.

Some of the older guys laughed when I shared this dilemma. They told me of an old combat trick: piss bottles. I was to save a few empty water bottles and urinate in them at night so that I didn't have to leave the concrete-covered room. I thought they were lying to me. I was used to being told some of the most sensationalized stories because it was also an old Army pastime to see who could shock the chaplain's sensibilities. Wanting to save myself the chagrin of being blown up in a pool of urine, I asked around. Sure enough, it was a common war hack. The only word of caution given to me was that I couldn't be lazy with the process. I needed to throw away the bottles the next day or they would start stinking. I asked them if they kept hand sanitizer next to the bed for afterward, and they looked at me like I was a diva. I tried it one night. I checked to make sure my roommate was asleep, and I went for it. Relieving myself in a bottle with another adult sleeping four feet away was foul. I could not do it. I would not do it. So, with a prayer, I steadied myself each night for the route to the latrine.

And then one day I discovered that I was accustomed to it all. I walked to the latrine no matter the hour with one eye closed and fell back to sleep within minutes of my return. It helped that the sirens rarely went off. Aside from the base defense drills, our warning sirens only went off one more time during the deployment, and that was from an accidental gun discharge. Over time, I learned that most of the errant gunfire comes from bored Iraqi security guards shooting at stray dogs. I came to trust so much and so completely in the training of those charged with my safety that I even began to speculate whether I was safer in Taji than my family was back in the States. I tried to fight this new paradigm. I knew that it should not seem normal, but within a few weeks the bubble of my FOB was my new reality.

From this context, I lived into my identity as a chaplain. I learned quickly that I was an embedded presence of hope. For those in uniform, I sought to be as constant as God's *hesed*, the steadfast presence of God's love. Unless I shut myself up in my room, there were no off moments, and even then, the knocks on my door would carry news that drew me back out into the world of my calling.

When I was being recruited for the Army Reserve in 2011, the concept of embeddedness was a selling feature. I vividly remember the conversation with the recruiter.

"You are an embedded asset," the recruiter stated.

Fascinated, I thought, *What does that even mean?*

Anticipating my thoughts, he continued, "You go where they go, eat what they eat, march where they march, and sleep where they sleep." The recruiter barked these words. Clearly, he had used these lines before. I smiled.

In the Army, I was assigned a unit as a battalion chaplain. It was an entry-level position. As advertised, where they moved, I tagged along. The Army didn't ask me to sit in a chapel all day waiting for people to stop by the office, which was what I had imagined that I would be doing before joining. I'd watched M*A*S*H. I loved Father Mulcahy. He hung out in his tent most of the time and proffered wisdom when the situation came to him. He was a sage, an oasis of holy in the middle of all that is not holy. I thought most people imagined that all Army chaplains were like the one portrayed on that show. I figured I would be a mix between Hawkeye Pierce and the gentle, turtlenecked chaplain, but one that actually ministered to all the soldiers, including the LGBT ones.

The modern chaplain was different. The Army needed more from this role in order to be effective. We were to ensure the constitutional right of free exercise of religion. We were there to nurture the living, care for the wounded, and honor the dead. We were there to advise the chain of command ethically and morally. Our effectiveness was measured by our capacity to embed with the soldiers under our care. I was enamored with the concept. In my civilian pastorate, I had similarly conceptualized that my vocation at Saguaro was also embedded within the broader Tucson community. I preached that the church was there for the community instead of assuming that the community was there for the church: "We are to be a church of the community and not just a church in the community." The Army had seemed the perfect fit if I was going to do this.

"Embedded?" I wryly quipped to the recruiter. "It sounds like being a counselor at a high school church camp!"

Not amused, he gritted out, "Except that the men and women alongside whom you'll be serving have been trained to kill."

Never one to shy away from an opportunity to be witty, I replied, "I get it. So, you are saying it's more like being a counselor at a middle school church camp. Good call." I still can't believe they offered me a commission!

That conversation with the recruiter now seemed so distant—as distant as those first few nights in Iraq, as distant as the disorientation of those first moments in theater, as distant as when I last saw my family.

I looked at the toilet and the counters, and said to the soldier, "Take a seat. Let's talk."

Even in deployments where the rockets and mortars were not perpetually showering their red glare, it was tough. The days and the distance and the fears ripped at the seams of families. We had been at war too long. I learned that quickly, especially as I counseled guys like this who had made multiple trips to Iraq. It was not necessarily the danger that wears the soldier, but the powerful, slow mix of the perception of danger and a duty description with no off button. For the sergeant who sat next to me, the details of our conversation did not matter. He was another man whose family was being torn asunder by America's perpetual war on terrorism. All he knew was that one text message had changed his life more than any of the enemies outside of the gates. All he knew was where his wife's breaking point was, but now that information would not really matter in the future. All he knew was that there would not be a home to go to.

Our conversation did not take too long, maybe twenty minutes. All I did was listen. He just needed someone to be present to honor his pain. That was most of what I did in Iraq. I stayed present in the uncertainty to remind them that this was not in fact normal—that God would meet them anywhere (even next to a nasty toilet)—and keep them whole. I was the sticky, sweating embodiment of God's hesed, for as the psalmist wrote, "Where can I go from your Spirit? Where can I flee from your presence?"

I almost peed my shorts that night. When I finally made it to my favorite stall, it was a moment of grace. I had been doing everything I could to keep my second eye from opening on that night, but God needed both of them open. It took two awakened eyes to see a moment for mercy. That was what embeddedness required of a chaplain.

After ten years of ordained ministry, it was humbling to realize how moments like this one in a latrine showed how much more there was to learn about ministry. The soldiers did not care that I could run a church or manage a staff. Most of them did not care about the God I called on in my times of prayer or the grace I tried to interject into our war-torn spaces. In Iraq, I was repeatedly tested in this battle of whether I would answer the familiar call—"Hey! Chaplain!"—and stand with a man or woman in the middle of their pain, no matter what foul smells seeped from closed stalls.

I walked back to my room tragically alert, but deeply fulfilled. On nights like this, the love of Christ whispered back to my fears, "You shall fear no evil," and my dreams were filled with the laughter of my children. I was one more sweaty day closer to them. Thanks be to God.

Chapter 4

Encounter with Fear:
A Moment in the Porta-Potty

I grew up fixated on the great war movies of the 1980s, as did my friends. I can still remember these B movies, with their gratuitous explosions and automatic gunfire and plenty of Cold War propaganda to weave it all together. We swallowed it all whole and chased it down with as much RC Cola as we could handle. The movie would end heroically and with chants of "USA! USA!" My friends and I would race out into the streets on our bikes, now transformed into tanks or helicopters, in order to recreate the glory. It was magnificent ... Well, unless you were on the losing end of "rock, paper, scissors," which cast you in the role of the Russians. There was no fun in being the Russians. That meant the next few hours of your life consisted of being killed, captured, or worse: tortured by wedgies.

We spent hours recreating the scenes in our mind. We pretended that the bombs of our enemies were being dropped on our position as we grandly took cover, sheltering our friends selflessly from its fires and percussions. Over and over again, we reenacted slow-motion dives as the sirens screeched, declaring our impending doom. We piled pillows that we dragged out from our bedrooms to form sandbags for our return fire. Then at some point the streetlights would come on and our pillows would return home, much like the soldiers they'd protected, covered in dirt and honor and the very real possibility that our mothers were going to kill us when they saw all the filth. These were some of my favorite memories of childhood.

These moments formed most, if not all, of the preconceived notions that I had about war in general. These days of play, testosterone, and prepubescent male bonding formed my embedded theology of geopolitical conflict and unified land war theory. Wars were short, filled with action, and the good guys always won.

And then the sirens went off for real in Iraq, by surprise, and without pretense, warning, or clear direction. This was my moment. This was when the director would scream, "Action!" The soundtrack would blare a choreographed mix of aggression and poise. This would be the event by which I defined my courage. But there was a problem: I was stuck in a Porta-Potty.

How nonsensical was that?

Initially, the sirens in Camp Taji that day weren't as loud as I figured that they would be in a moment like this. In fact, I wasn't even sure whether I was really hearing what I thought that I was hearing. The heat and the fumes were creating enough self-doubt that I remember pausing from my business and cracking the door a sliver in order to get a clearer understanding of the commotion. Unmistakably, the loudspeakers crowed, "Take cover ... Indirect fire ... Take cover!" On and on, the speaker blared this message so loudly that, at this point, I couldn't hear anything over it once my mind had locked on to the alert.

Panic set in quickly. Our bodies really are marvelous. Adrenaline spread throughout my body within a few slowed breaths. Within a second of the crackle of the special speaker, my heart was pumping at an unnerving primordial speed. I could hear my own pulse. Every detail around me came into a surreal visual and olfactory clarity, which, considering the current context of my setting, was less than ideal. I rapidly made a thousand different calculations of possible egress and regress plans as I sorted through all of my military training, but I was stuck. Instead of galloping toward defensive fortification as clouds of fire balls exploded around me in an homage to the movies of my childhood, I, embarrassingly, was immobilized as I had the excrement literally scared out of me.

Nature called before duty did that day, and there I was on a gross, sticky, unbearably hot, plastic throne. There was no glossing over it. It was not a fortified position. There was not anything special that would protect it or me if a mortar landed anywhere close. There were no turrets to return fire if needed. Most soldiers couldn't even get their guns to fit in the space with them as they relieved themselves. Typically, they would have their battle buddy hold their weapon when they went in to do their business, or if they were close enough to their TOCs, they would just leave them next to their desks. Nope. Nothing military about it. This Porta-Potty was just like the ones used at fairs or concerts back home, replete with adolescent male graffiti.

My mind was preparing for a fight-or-flight decision as the sirens continued to sound, but my bowels were still locked into a post-lunch disagreement with the tuna I had chosen. I felt silly, certainly not heroic. I prayed that they would never make a movie of this moment. In my heart of hearts, I knew that I wouldn't have made it against the Russians. I never once saw Rambo stop, even to urinate.

Taking stock of where I was, I knew that the closest bunker was two hundred yards away. I could be there in less than a minute ... probably sooner, given my current motivation.

We had been told that a typical IDF situation would last only a few moments—no more than a minute or so. I had been told the enemy would often rig a series of hidden mortars on the rooftops of surrounding neighborhoods. They would light a fuse or rig a remote device and then retreat, disappearing into the local population, as the mortars discharged indiscriminately. They were less concerned with accuracy than with letting US forces know that they could hit them. As I understood it, ISIS would be long gone before any of our military forces could apprehend them. Though this system was ingenious at preventing capture, it lacked any accuracy or intention. It was random and absurd, but it created fear because anything could be a target at any moment, even a Porta-Potty adjacent to a chapel, which held no military value.

In my present situation, I figured thirty seconds had already passed. I was still in immediate danger, though I could hear no booms over the sirens. We were drilled on these scenarios bimonthly in Taji. When the sirens stopped, my goal was to make it to the hospital to help provide religious support to the wounded and dead. I tried to recollect whether there would be a different siren if this was a chemical gas attack. It would not matter anyway. My gas mask and chemical suit were in my CHU. We all kept them there as an afterthought. Considering my mask had been lost when it was shipped over to Iraq and the one that they had given me didn't fit my face, I figured there was not much I could do even if we were under a gas attack.

Fear overwhelmed me. I cursed my indecisiveness and the timing of my bowels. I reckoned that I could make a run for the nearest bunker. That seemed to be the smart play. I could just pull up my pants, give them a quick button up, and go. I would try not to think about the lack of hygiene or the physical restraint this all required. Additionally, I would have to make peace with the probable scenario in which I would be trapped in a bunker with other soldiers until the "all clear" sirens signaled an end to the bombardment, which could take hours, with a soiled uniform.

In my head, I could hear a voice say, *Run! For God's sake, take cover!* I imagined that was what anyone's voice would be saying. But I couldn't do it. I just couldn't bring myself to leave. I stayed in the Porta-Potty. The fact remained that I was actively vacating my lunch, and I had no desire to poop myself in a hot, dusty bunker in front of a gaggle of twenty-year-olds. I held my ground as I waited and listened to the sounds of my possible endangerment. It was absurd. The whole thing. I know it was, but it was what I did.

And so, my mind drifted into the absurdity. Fear was strange that way.

I didn't know what I thought a soldier would think about in moments like this. As kids we didn't debrief each other throughout the battle to check on our emotional complexities. I am sure I speculated about fear at some point, but my inner dialogue defied me. I knew I was scared, but this fear didn't feel like I thought it would feel. It wasn't suffocating, like your breath was being stolen from you. I do not even remember it being terrifying. I didn't close my eyes with despair or wash out the noise with cries. That moment of fear just felt slow, almost like time was fighting with itself on whether to proceed.

A couple of years before this deployment to Iraq, I had sat with some of the last remaining veterans of WWII in Saguaro's congregation. I wanted to hear their stories before it was too late. I created a sermon series on selfless service and fear around Veterans Day. I centered the whole series on the scripture "don't fear those things that can kill the body, but can't kill the soul." This had always been one of my favorite scriptures from the gospels. I remembered naïvely holding these words within my heart as a justification for joining the military. From these sacred words of Christ, I found the courage to be—to be what God called me to be—and the courage to trust—to trust in the power of our spiritual identity with God and each other in uniform.

Turning to these old veterans, I asked them if they remembered being scared at any point during their time in theater. How had they gotten through it? Each veteran had a different story. They spoke of their experiences as if they were as vivid as the day they had happened. I could see it in the distant look their eyes took on in the telling. In the gift of each conversation, there was a common theme that emerged within this absurdity. Each recounted saying a prayer, permitting their minds to protect them, and then executing what they needed to do. They all made specific mention of time slowing down and speeding up simultaneously. I wondered whether God had wrapped their experiences in the thin spaces between time and the eternal.

It was silly, really. I listened to their stories, but I never made the connection that if I were to have a similar experience that somehow my experience of this prime emotion would be the same. I didn't know why I thought my experience of fear would be different. I could chalk it up to a common fallacy many ministers embody: We love to believe we live intentionally deep existences worthy of perpetual sermon fodder that sets us apart. In hindsight, it was safe to theorize that my misperceptions of fear sitting in that Porta-Potty were the product of my war illusions and the emotional distance ministers create in order to maintain a pastoral perspective.

The absurdity of these thoughts stirred as the words drummed on: "Indirect fire ... Take cover ... Indirect fire!" By this point, the sirens were so loud that I couldn't hear anything else in that Porta-Potty. I unknowingly reckoned there would be the footsteps of rushing soldiers, the engines of responding rapid response teams, or the shouts of humanity unable to solve their conflicts without bloodshed. I didn't hear any of this. I kept listening, thinking that my mind was playing tricks on me, but my preconceived notions weren't running around the battle space. There were sirens, and there were my thoughts enveloped in fear. "They cannot kill your soul, Owen," I said over and over again.

Fear was powerful. As I sat in the disgustingness of that place, my mind drifted to home. I could see my whole family, but my focus locked on to my daughters, specifically my daughter Eleanor. I could see her. I could hear her. She was at the kitchen table. I could even feel the table where she had sawed it with a knife when she was younger. She was standing on the leg supports of the chair, rocking it back and forth, which drove me absolutely nuts because she had already broken one chair doing the same thing.

Eleanor was having a familiar argument with her older sister, Harper, about who was really the oldest. For the record, Harper was almost exactly two years older than Eleanor, but there's a catch to the story. We named Eleanor after my best friend and post-seminary roommate, an American bulldog named Eleanor Roosevelt. She was the best dog I had ever had. We'd done everything together. Our favorite moments included drinking beer (she was a Miller Lite girl) and watching the Kentucky Wildcats play basketball. She was whimsical, funny, and tough as nails, but she was flawed. Her hips gave out on her too soon, which caused a way-too-early journey to the rainbow bridge. This all occurred around the time that Harper was born.

The way the story goes was that when Emily was pregnant with our second child, we were struggling with a name. Our pattern was that we always picked a boy's name and a girl's name because we never learned the sex of the baby prior to birth. We figured there were so few surprises left in the world, why ruin this one? We also learned early on that trying to name a baby was the quickest way to hurt the feelings of one's extended family. We created a system in which we selected a first name that we liked that was historically significant and a middle name that honored our family.

Emily's pregnancy with our second child was difficult, however. Emily was in a bad car accident; she was in a horrible, bullying work environment; and we were almost carbon monoxide poisoned after a negligent furnace installation. Through it all, the baby inside thrived. One night, after a few too many Shiner beers and a sentimental movie featuring Matt Damon, I pleaded with Emily that if our second child was a girl that we should name her after the two strongest women I had ever known: Eleanor, the bulldog, and Virginia, my saint of a grandmother. Eleanor Virginia Chandler was born as defiantly as her namesakes.

Now, somewhere along the line (and I know that I probably had a great deal to do with it), Eleanor, our daughter, became convinced that she was once the bulldog, Eleanor. She even referred to old photos of the dog as "the puppy Eleanor." The way the tale continued was this: Eleanor the puppy was such a good friend to me that God came down and turned the puppy into a child, my daughter. Cute, right? Sometimes, I would catch her in my office looking at a photo I keep of Eleanor, the bulldog. "I really was so adorable when I was a puppy!" So, in Eleanor's mind, since she was a puppy before Harper was born, logic clearly dictated that Eleanor was the oldest of the two, even though she hadn't been human as long.

I sat in that Porta-Potty and listened to them argue, and I smiled. The whole moment felt like forever, but it probably only lasted a minute, maybe two. As I smiled, I didn't feel the fear anymore. I am sure it was still there. I was not superhuman, but I don't remember it as being as all-consuming. Love had quieted my fear. Love protected my soul. It was the love blessed by God, shared by Christ, and carried within the spirit which traverses the most intimate places our being and experience.

So how did the Porta-Potty story end?

I finished, and by the time I started running for the bunkers, the sirens had just stopped. Even though the threat was no longer active, it did not mean we were able to resume our daily activities. We had to wait for the "all clear" siren, which would tell us that threat was over or that it had been neutralized. There was no timetable on this type of operation. One was expected to be patient and ready.

I ran for the bunker, where I sat with other soldiers for an hour or so, waiting for the "all clear" siren. They were so young and visibly scared. They had been on their way to the gym, and so they were ill-prepared for this moment too. They sat holding their

M16s while clothed in their physical fitness uniforms complete with reflector safety belts. We sat in that hot space and I told them funny stories and I made fun of their moms. With each laugh, the fear on their faces dissipated.

Eventually, the siren declaring our safety was sounded. In the aftermath, I was taught another timeless lesson about war: It was preposterously random and often accidental. There was an unpredictable quality to a combat zone that was seldom portrayed on the big screen. I didn't know whether it was because it made for a bad story in that there really wasn't a driving narrative in which one moment builds to the next, or whether it was just because it was difficult to capture the off-speed nature of moments like this one. The truth of my experience is that I spent 99.9 percent of my time doing normal things like using the restroom, sending emails, and waiting in lines for food. When danger crossed our path at Camp Taji, there was no way of knowing until it happened.

As a result, a chronic hyperalertness cut with a healthy dose of complacency began to shape most of my days there. Typically, this meant that a situation would go from a constant low-grade level to an emergency in an instant. This reality allowed us to function as we were tasked to, but also to be instantly mission capable if called on. This also meant that small mistakes regularly got blown way out of proportion.

For example, the afternoon on which I contemplated my death within the sacred walls of a Porta-Potty, the sirens had been a gaffe. A team of US engineers was building an extension to a runway. There was an errant burst of gunfire from an Iraqi training team learning how to clean a .50-caliber machine gun. The gunfire was probably a mile away from the engineers, but in the fear-induced confusion, one of the US soldiers knocked over a cone on the construction site. When he turned around, he saw a mortar lodged in the concrete. The leaders assumed that the gunfire and the mortar were connected and had set off the sirens, while a tragically pale chaplain was in a Porta-Potty lamenting his choice in sandwiches.

The story got even better. Turns out the mortar had been there for over a year. When it landed and failed to explode, a soldier placed a cone on it so that the explosive ordnance disposal (EOD) team would know where to find it. Unfortunately, someone had forgotten to tell the EOD about the cone. For over a year, people had walked by the cone, assuming that someone else had placed it there for a reason, and left it alone. Then one unit switched with another unit, and then that unit switched with another unit. All the while the cone remained, until that one fateful day when a soldier accidentally tripped over the unexploded mortar in fear of an accident miles away.

I could not think of a better parable for these drawn-out wars. This was probably why Hollywood hadn't made any over-the-top war movies about Iraq. Oh, what would our nation's youth do if they could grow up idolizing war like my generation did?

Chapter 5

The Coalition Forces: A Funny Story

I love a good story.

When studying scripture, I am drawn to the great storytellers of my sacred texts. I love the books of Genesis and Judges. I am shocked, inspired, and moved by the characters of these ancient accounts. The depth of my relationship with Jesus has been formed and fostered by the parables he shared with those who gathered at his feet. I am humbled by his capacity to create sacred space and hope among his people using anecdotes woven from their shared traditions. I could sit for hours listening to retired ministers reliving experiences of how the living word of God spoke to the living stories of God's children during their ministerial walks. Yes, I love a good story!

Growing up in Kentucky, I was surrounded by folks who could take you on unbelievable narrative journeys. Along the way, I learned that ornery men were especially gifted in this art (and there was no short supply of those in my family). The capacity to tell a good yarn was a form of cultural currency. Someone quick with a remembrance and a quip was granted access to almost any table. It bridged social and economic classes. It created pathways between the bulwarks of political ideology. It ignited romantic relationships and it undergirded lifelong friendships. When it came time to leave Kentucky to follow my call, I did not leave with much money, but I left with a barn load of stories and a few good ideas on how to share them.

Throughout my ministerial journey, I have leaned on the twist of an unexpected plot. It has served me well over the years, though I sometimes wonder whether it was a crutch or a defense mechanism. I don't know. Storytelling has given me tools to communicate grace-filled moments that I did not have any other capacity to share. I joke with friends when they ask what it's like to minister to a church in Arizona. I tell them, "Kentucky translates well in the desert." I thought my subtle southern accent added a little humidity to the sagas I shared. I have subsequently learned that it translated well within the military chaplaincy, too, and probably for the same reason. I have discovered that even the most grizzled command sergeant major can be softened with an especially humorous story.

In Iraq, a good story nearly always found a willing home. How could it not? There was so much administrative monotony within a combat theater. By the end of our time in Iraq, we had soldiers who previously could barely type with two fingers morphing into Excel and Outlook professionals. They even joked that they were the Special Forces of Microsoft Office, regular PowerPoint Rangers. In an environment like this, soldiers were more than willing to give you their full attention if it meant that they could take a break from their work for a while. There was one unit that even set up cornhole boards once a week so that I would stop by to chat, tell stories, and hustle cornhole.

Camp Taji was a coalition forces FOB. I felt as if we were stationed in a global village. We were home to four coalition military partners: the Brits, the Aussies, the Kiwis (New Zealanders), and the Spaniards. This last group mostly kept to themselves because of the language barrier and because they were a true special forces unit. In fact, they had their own compound within the compound that required special clearances to access that I didn't have. Also on Taji were contracted personnel from Fiji and the Philippines. All of these entities, including US forces, were housed and operated within an area that was maybe six city blocks. With our movements constricted and our views limited to the twenty-foot concrete barriers (or T-walls) that caged us, the military partners were able to get to know each other. I quickly learned that stories are a universal currency that can help create bridges between nations and gain access to some interesting scenes.

For example, within the battle rhythm of Camp Taji there emerged a social rhythm to the FOB too. Sometimes these nightly gatherings were posted and promoted, like the occasional volley-ball tournament or poker night, but many of them were informal. There were groups that watched rugby and others that met to lift and grunt during powerlifting hangouts at the gym. These happenings provided needed diversion during the repetitive routine of deployment, where it was often difficult to know what day it was because all the days were basically the same.

Then there were "in-the-know" parties. These were invitation-only scenes. They were not as scandalous as one might imagine. For a start, alcohol and drugs were prohibited. If a soldier was caught drinking, it would turn into an automatic Field Grade Article 15, which could end a career. Occasionally I would hear rumors that alcohol had been bootlegged, and once we had someone break into the chapel and steal all the sacramental wine, so I am not so naïve as to think that there were not some shady things happening on Taji. No, most of these private gatherings were of senior officers, wary of the appearance of fraternization, who organized cigar-smoking nights between other field grade officers. As a captain, I was rarely invited to these events.

Luckily, I stumbled upon a regular, invite-only Friday night movie party with some of the Australian medical teams early on in our deployment. I had befriended the Australian officer-in-charge (OIC) of the clinic early on after regular visits to check on his team's well-being.

The Major was a storyteller. I picked up on that right away.

"Padre, where are you from?" he asked one afternoon.

The Major was a handsome fella, kind of like a rich man's Gary Sinise. To be fair, all the Australians were stunning, much to the anguish of the young male US soldiers who were competing with them for the attention of the few single female soldiers. I used to laugh at the number of "tough" guys who took every sniffle to the beautiful female Australian nurses.

"Originally, I am from Kentucky. Do you know where that is?"

"Of course. Every bourbon drinker knows where that is. Besides, you forget that only Americans are ignorant of geography.

For instance, I am from Brisbane. Do you know where that is?" he baited me.

"Absolutely, it's in Australia," I stated quickly. He laughed.

Truthfully, I was mortified. I routinely met people from the coalition presence and had absolutely no idea where the city was that they claimed as home. I made a practice of making a quick note and then pulling up a map on the Internet when I got back to the office. One day, I came upon an old quote from Mark Twain that read, "God created war so that Americans would learn geography." This thought hit a little too close to home!

"It's funny, because for the longest time, everything I knew about Australia I picked up from Looney Tunes. You know ... the Tasmanian devil and the boxing kangaroo?" I laughingly offered.

"Ha! Well, then you know everything you need to know about Australia!" He paused. "I was the same with the States when I was a kid. I just loved those Road Runner and Wile E. Coyote cartoons!" The Major was laughing at the memory.

"Ha! That's actually where I live now—in Tucson, Arizona." I laughed. "There's a roadrunner that runs along my fence most mornings looking for lizards, and there's a pack of coyotes in the open land behind our house."

"What? Seriously?"

"Yep, every morning you can hear the roadrunner plodding along the top of the fencerow."

"Seriously? How do you hear them?" His voice grew louder.

"Because they go 'Beep! Beep!'" I tried to say it without a hint of mischief.

A few seconds, and then there was a cascading rush of laughter.

"Padre! What about the coyotes?"

"Since we have a fire ban due to drought conditions, it has really limited their use of rockets. I kind of feel for them. It's like we took away their purpose. So kangaroos don't really box, then? I feel like my childhood might have been a lie."

"Actually, kangaroos are real assholes, the whole lot of them."

He invited me to stop back later that night to watch a movie in the beer garden. I had heard about the beer garden, but I didn't know it actually existed. I assumed it was a legend where near beer flowed like honey and the doctors sat around remarking on how much more beautiful they were compared to the rest of Camp Taji. Turns out it was a real place tucked behind the helipad and the clinic. Each Friday, they paused for cigar smoking and old 1980s American comedies, like *Ghostbusters*.

I returned later that night with some near beer tucked under my arms and a cigar dangling from my lips. At first, I could not find the place. I didn't really see how to get behind the clinic. As I wandered around cluelessly, I laughed at the thought of a beer garden nestled in Taji. The entire FOB looked like a scene out of a cheap postapocalyptic movie. Many of the buildings were left bombed out from the original invasion when this military installation was home to Saddam's tanks and his chemical weapons. In fact, the Australians took daily air samples because they were concerned that the dust we inhaled might be tinged with chemical residues.

I eventually found a broken sidewalk that curved around the building. As I walked around, I began to smell the smoke and hear the laughter. I turned the corner to find a quaint and clever beer garden. It was lit with white Christmas lights, which created an almost homey atmosphere. There were tables with plastic tablecloths and plastic patio chairs like the ones that provide comfort to millions of Americans every summer. Around each table, doctors, nurses, commanders, regular soldiers from across the coalition, and even a few contractors sat enthralled in conversation.

I kept thinking I'd been magically transported into an episode of M*A*S*H set in Iraq.

"Padre!" a familiar voice called out as he pulled out a chair.

I turned and saw the Major sitting with military personnel I recognized from different places. I took the seat, and as I did, one of the guys sitting at the table slid me a Velcro patch. "Camp Taji Combat Cigar Club." I placed it on my uniform that night and many other Friday nights to come. I was not a smoker before the deployment, and my wife frequently remarked that some habits should stay in Iraq.

Those Friday nights became a place of hospitality, deep conversation, and storytelling. It was fascinating to discuss world events from the perspectives of worldly people. Critical thinking, engaging ideas, and humorous candor were the common thread. Many a Friday night I sat around that table humbled by the magnitude and insight of the conversations.

I remember the exchange we had the night after we watched *Caddyshack*. It began a conversation that carried over several more Friday nights.

"Americans used to make such great movies, and then you got so sexually uptight and insecure," a British soldier remarked.

"What do you mean?" I asked. As a tall, often doughy, pale-faced redhead who hadn't hit puberty until age seventeen, I was well acquainted with sexual insecurity. I had a hard time imagining that the movie we'd just watched, loaded with objectification, somehow represented a treatise of healthy sexuality.

"You are so afraid of sex. But all it really does is take away the healthy ways to be human and transfer all that energy into inappropriate dark corners," a Kiwi responded.

"I think it's why you all stay so busy all the time! So that you don't think about your bodies or sex or all that other natural stuff that seems to embarrass the lot of you." The Brit grinned.

One of the Australian nurses laughed at this.

"Have you ever seen a nation that just relishes creating work for themselves?" she added and they all laughed.

Minus our prudish impulses, I figured that they were on to something. I had just returned from a Spanish FOB in Besmaya, Iraq. There was a small US presence there to help with the logistics of the training mission. Since it was such a small company, a chaplain had not been placed with them, and so I rode the Chinook out there during the middle of the night to offer basic religious services and any counseling that might be needed.

The European posts were considerably different than the US bases. On my first day in Besmaya, I went to use the restroom, which also served as a shower point. I walked into the facility sleepily. I turned to the left when I saw the urinals and proceeded to vacate my bladder, as we say in Kentucky. (No one actually says this.)

As I stood there, I heard a shower stall door open behind me. Out of my periphery, I watched as a woman adjusted her towel, smiled, and offered a simple greeting in Spanish. Immediately I panicked. As I painfully attempted to stop the stream and button up my pants, my mind raced. I imagined the Article 15: Perverted Chaplain Caught in Women's Shower Facilities. Back at Taji, the women's showering facilities were locked with a code that only female personnel could access.

I was so confused. There were urinals in front of me, but clearly there was also a Spanish-speaking woman asking me about my day and wearing only a white towel as she put on her makeup. I buttoned my uniform before I could finish urinating, which created a laundry situation for later that day. As I was running out, I bumped into a US soldier. I asked him harshly to direct me to the nearest men's restroom. He looked at me bewildered. I double-checked his uniform to make sure he was one of ours and then asked him the question again. Slowly, he raised his finger and pointed at the place from which I had just emerged. Aghast, I turned around.

"Everything is coed here and shit." He stumbled over the words. "I just tell my soldiers to keep their eyes on the road when they go in."

I shared my story at the table in that enchanted beer garden.

"Padre! That's a great story!" The Major chortled. Everyone laughed.

"I always love having a great chaplain on post," one of the Australian commanders offered.

"What about a bad chaplain?" the Major asked.

"I'll take a great padre into war any day. Even if it means I have to leave behind a gunman." He took a drag on his cigar. "A great padre is worth their weight in gold. They can influence all the intangibles of courage on which a commander relies for success on the battlefield. A bad padre just gets in the way and wastes a unit's time."

Those at the table nodded their heads. I realized I was hearing one of the best definitions of chaplaincy and what we bring to the fight.

I pondered his response for a moment. As a chaplain, I was often asked to provide a thought to frame the start of a meeting. It was called the "Word of the Day." I always took the opportunities seriously even as I often interjected humor into what I said. I wanted our soldiers to think, to consider, and to feel. I strove to expose them to as many authors, artists, theologians, and philosophers as possible.

There, under the white patio lights, I shared with the table a passage I had used earlier that month:

"The true soldier fights not because he hates what is in front of him, but because he loves what is behind him." G. K. Chesterton.

The table sat and considered the idea. They patiently drew upon their cigars and rolled the thought over in their minds. I loved this about the group. There was no rush to fill a void with the first thing that spilled out of their minds. As an American and a minister, I typically felt the need to respond as quickly as possible.

"I feel like part of my role as chaplain is to create a deeper reflection of a soldier's humanity, but then I wonder if it complicates the war by making the soldier less of a machine and more of a soul," I said.

"I can promise you that they aren't machines. I've been doing this for a long time. We've been doing this for a long time. They aren't machines ..." The Australian nurse's voice trailed off as she looked around the table.

The Australian commander put down his cigar.

"I think that's the hardest part about this ongoing war. It's easy to forget why you are here. It's easy to forget that many of our brothers and sisters have died in this place where we now sit. We owe it to them to do our best."

We let the commander's words rest there.

I don't know why, but I thought about Jesus later that night as I captured the group's thoughts in my journal. I thought about the disciples. I thought about the early church. I thought about how crucial it became to tell the stories of grace, especially as the message of God's redemptive love spread to all the places around the world that were starved of hope. I figured that was what a good story does—it connects people through time and space so that a shared future is possible. I prayed that I was living through a similar story.

"I bet the Iraqis have stories like this. I wonder when we will all get to share them." And with that, the Major stubbed out his cigar, and we called it a night.

"Beep beep," I mumbled to myself as I went home.

Chapter 6

The Witness of War:
I Saw Satan Fall like Lightning

"Are you always in your head?"

"Always." I smiled. At least, I tried to smile. It probably looked more like a grimace.

"Does it ever do you any good?"

"Seldom."

Over in the corner of the PAX terminal of the troop transportation airport there was a dog, a German Shepherd or maybe a Belgian Malinois. It captured my attention as it danced and played with its handler. A real smile crept onto my face. I climbed to my feet, dropped my pack, and headed over to get a closer look at the dog.

As I walked closer, the dog presented a play bow. The handler laughed. I laughed. This was the first dog I had seen in months. I felt joy even as I felt exhausted. I had been sitting on the concrete of this PAX terminal in Baghdad for over an hour, mostly watching this dog. This wasn't unusual. Well, the dog part was. That's what I did as I awaited troop transport; I waited, and I waited, and I waited.

Just two hours ago, I had been standing on a different airstrip way out west in Anbar province. I was preparing for movement back to Taji by hitching a ride on a C-130 back to Baghdad and then hopefully making a helicopter hop over to Taji. We had tried this maneuver unsuccessfully every other night for over a week, but high winds and ongoing missions in the area had prevented our exit.

I had not minded the delay due to the experiences it provided. For example, the time afforded me the opportunity to meet and befriend another chaplain in my denomination. We had several mutual friends, but we had never crossed paths before. He was a generous spirit and had a wealth of experience. He shared many stories of life within this Marine-operated FOB as we sat and smoked pipes.

Whereas most of the FOBs in Iraq were operated by the Army, occasionally you would come across one that was supported either by another branch or by a coalition partner. It didn't take any time at all to discover that the FOBs operated by the Air Force were the nicest. They just knew how to do things. The food was better, and the Wi-Fi was infinitely more stable.

It also didn't take any time to learn that the Marine-operated FOBs excelled at creating as austere an atmosphere as possible. They took a person's discomfort as a sense of pride. For example, at this installation I was required to fill two sandbags prior to entering the mess hall. Another example: There were no CHUs. Instead, there were large, shared tents with HVAC systems that either melted me or froze me depending on the season. There was a single Wi-Fi spot that had sporadic service. The dozens of marines and soldiers huddling around it like gazelles around a desert oasis made it easy to find.

During my stay there, my friend and I were able to provide chapel together. It was one of my most memorable experiences. There, at that distant outpost, I stood beside him and we celebrated communion together. This was a sacred moment for me. Christ's broken body and blood filled the space of this broken place. As I listened to him pray, I wondered if Jesus had ever imagined that that night in the upper room would still be so needed thousands of years later.

There were advantages to being stuck there. The delay formed the backdrop to the only real brush with coolness I had on the deployment. The operational tempo was slow at the moment, and so most nights there was a pickup basketball game. It was run by some Navy SEALs. These guys were athletic freaks of nature. The majority of them were as tall as me, but they were powerful, agile, and quick. I played my way into the game and did well enough that I was welcomed to play each night I was there.

Over the course of a few days, I was invited to their table at mealtime. I listened to their stories, their laments, and their thoughts. The entire time I sat there, I kept thinking, *Be cool, be cool, be cool, for God's sake, Owen, don't be a dork.* Basically, I had nightmares of middle school all over again. It was intoxicating and terrifying, but fortunately they kept inviting me back.

By the end of that stopover, I joked with them one night after basketball.

"Guys, make me a promise."

I put a serious face on for the moment.

"When they make the eventual movie about you guys, be sure to include a random chaplain that plays basketball with you during one of the scenes. I want to be able to tell my kids that the lanky guy in the back was their dad!" They laughed.

One of the principal reasons for the delay was ISIS. They were stuck in the desert. As I understood it, they had tried to use the winds to their advantage; the winds made it difficult for US forces to provide the Iraqis with much air support. In light of a losing situation in nearby Ramadi and Fallujah, a group of ISIS fighters had tried to sneak out in a caravan of a couple hundred vehicles. The front and rear cars were targeted by our forces, and this trapped them.

One day, as I tagged along with my chaplain friend as he made his rounds, we stopped into an operations room where the disabled caravan was on the screen from the feed of a drone circling above in the sky. I didn't understand much of the discussions of the teams there or what they intended to do with the remaining forces stranded in the desert. On the screen I could see the aerial view of the vehicles, especially the Toyota Hilux trucks, which seemed to be the official truck of ISIS. A few weeks prior, our unit had helped ship a dozen or so trucks to an Iraqi militia. About a week afterward, as we watched CNN, we saw a clip of ISIS fighters driving new Hiluxes that looked almost exactly like the ones we had just divested. Honestly, the scene on the screens of this operation center was so bizarre to me that I forgot about the situation almost as rapidly as we had strolled into it.

And then one night as we made camp in the PAX terminal, word finally came that I would be able to stow away on a flight back to Baghdad. Finally, I rejoiced. I needed to get back and check on my unit and the chapel on Taji. I grabbed my gear, put on my flak jacket and helmet, and lined up.

The ride out to the flight line was grave. All the lights on the vehicle were blacked out. In fact, the driver shuttled our group out the corridor using night vision goggles. Once we arrived at our point, the engine shut off, and the windows were rolled down since the heat was stifling in all of that gear.

A few minutes later, the roar of a plane was heard, but it was impossible to see anything in the night sky. As the tear of the engines crept closer, we were eventually able to see the outline of a C-130 emerge. It rolled to a stop, the rear hatch was lowered, and cargo was quickly loaded, all the while the engines remained engaged. We were given the signal to line up and move forward toward the rear of the plane, careful to stay out of the heat of the engines.

The sound of this plane was deafening even with earplugs firmly fixed. My eyes had adjusted to the night, and so I remained focused on the soldier ahead of me. We were maybe fifty yards from the plane when the line halted. We stayed there for about twenty minutes with no further instruction or even any explanation as to why we had been stalled. The noise from the plane stifled any conversation. I couldn't even hear myself think. As my eyes wandered the stars above, I dreamt of Tucson; we have the best night skies in the Sonoran Desert. While I searched for familiar constellations, I noticed a small flash in the not-too-distant sky. It struck me as a curiosity at first.

In a matter of seconds, the sky was violent and iridescent. The horizon filled with an erratic rhythm of light. It writhed within a torrent of haze. Darkness smothered each burst with death. And through it all, I heard absolutely nothing but the encompassing blare of airplane engines paused with what I had thought was no purpose. In my heart, I heard my soul speak: "And I saw Satan fall like lightning from heaven." I exhaled a few labored breaths. I had witnessed the last breaths of an enemy miles in the distance. It was finished. Targets eliminated.

A few more minutes passed, and eventually the signal was given to board the C-130. I wrestled with my gear as the soldier behind me nudged me forward. I battled my footing as I climbed into the cargo hold and folded my long legs up. Mostly, I fought with a thought that my new chaplain friend had posed: The role of the chaplain was to ask great questions so that a person had to entertain new ways in which God's voice was speaking to them. I felt that question before me as I continued a theological discussion with the Christ of my faith commanding me to love my enemies.

This tenet of the Christian faith was an unavoidable dilemma. I figured that at some point in my military chaplaincy I would have to wade through this conversation of whether I was loving my enemies by offering direct support to their destruction. Fortunately, this dialogue had remained an abstract one for most of my days in Iraq, but I had given it some thought.

Earlier in the deployment, I had been trapped in a ridiculous conversation. Captain Twin was holding court in a TOC in between one of the hundreds of daily briefings. He was surrounded by Specialists Mafia who were hanging on his every word as he regaled them with stories of his previous deployments and the many and varied dangers he and his unit had overcome.

"Every convoy I went on got blown up," he matter-of-factly stated to the wide eyes of the soldiers present. His class continued.

"You guys don't know what a real deployment is, sitting here like fobbits and shit."

I could see the eyes of these younger soldiers lower self-consciously. There was this perpetual drive to prove yourself, especially within the Reserve, especially in front of the soldiers who were prior-infantry or some other combat arms branch. I had sat through many of these "real deployment" conversations over the last several months.

I interjected, "So, you are saying that unless we suffer a TBI [traumatic brain injury] or some other wound, this deployment isn't a real deployment?"

"Basically."

I stared at him.

"I love you, but you are a fucking idiot," I said. The specialists laughed, but then stopped when the captain glared at them.

"If I get to go home without a TBI or PTSD ... If I get to go home with all my limbs ... If I get to go home without having to do a memorial service for any of you ... then I'm good with that," I finished.

He rolled his eyes at me. The young enlisted soldiers went back to their tasks. I grabbed another bottle of water from the fridge.

To be fair to the underlying point of the captain, we were fortunate. This was not the Iraq war of the beginning invasion or the surge. This was not the Taji of "Taji, a good place to go get mortared." We did not face a daily threat of that magnitude. In fact, after a few weeks in Iraq, I rarely had my chaplain assistant attached to me as I walked Taji. I felt he was better used completing organizational and administrative tasks than following me around with a gun all day. Outside of the airstrip in the Anbar province, I never witnessed another act of gross war or death. I was blessed.

The reality was that our operation sounded and smelled and felt differently than all the stories and movies. For me, war sounded like keystrokes on dust-caked keyboards. It smelled like dirty dudes trying to get one more day out of their uniform before doing laundry. There was an incessant background noise as scattered TVs within the TOCs drowned out ringing phones. There were endless junk food wrappers on desks and equally endless conversations about how this will be the week we get into shape.

All this was packed into a decaying, compact military post. It's weird how I got used to such a small place. The whole AO, or area of operation, we inhabited was no bigger than most of the prisons outside of Tucson, where many of the Reserve soldiers worked on the civilian side. After a short while, it started to feel normal. The routine, the sounds, the smells, the salutes, the food, the life—it was all ordinary.

Complacency seemed predestined, and it aggravated the staff section tasked with breaking us of this laxity. Every day we were given a threat brief as part of the overall battle update. Initially, I was terrified by this unavoidable ten minutes every morning. In my journals, I named this staff section the Harbinger of Hopelessness. These dudes reveled in giving us the worst-case scenarios. And these were definitely easy to come by where we were.

For starters, all of Iraq was distressed by the prospect of ISIS demolishing the Mosul Dam. An event like that would flood and sweep away significant population centers along the river, including our location. There were international teams working through courses of action if this infrastructure was to be targeted. We were hundreds of miles away, but if the dam collapsed, we could expect to be overwhelmed by ten feet of water in hours. Our battle rattle, the Kevlar, the helmets, the protective pouches, could not be used as flotation devices in such an event.

Additionally, at Taji we held ISIS prisoners. They were on the Iraqi side of the camp, but that didn't lessen my anxiety about their proximity. We were informed that ISIS operators maintained plans for a complex attack to free them. This, it was said, would unfold with an offensive in which a suicide bomber would blow up the front gate, and then another would simultaneously blow up another vulnerable place within the wall. During the melee, ISIS fighters would storm deeper within camp and launch another series of suicide attacks. A final group of ISIS fighters would target the prison in an attempt to free their soldiers.

I recall one week in particular when, during the actual battle update brief, the entire TOC shook with a boom. Everyone paused. There were no additional explosions. The battalion commander ordered soldiers to contact the base defense and surveillance teams and learn the situation. Minutes later, the soldiers briefed that the main gate, miles away on the Iraqi side of Taji, had been attacked by suicide bombers, but that there was no further engagement. That week there would be several more attempts on that front gate. Many Iraqi soldiers and contractors lost their lives, and there was a heightened sense of alarm.

Later that week, sometime in the early hours of morning, my roommate and I were jarred awake by the rattling of our CHU. If he was unnerved by the noise, he didn't show it. I watched him as my eyes adjusted to the darkness. He was sitting up, but he was not out of his bed. It was difficult to hear anything because of the loud hum of a worn-out air-conditioner on its last legs. I listened for any additional explosions, but there were none. I could hear my pulse in my ears. There were no sirens indicating defensive postures. It was unsettling. I watched as he lowered himself back into his bed. I did the same. I wrestled with sleep the rest of the night.

The next day, we learned that the EOD and their Iraqi counterparts had located an improvised explosive device (IED) factory just outside of our walls, probably less than a mile from where we were sleeping. They had neutralized the operation, and that was what had created the detonation. There was a sense of elation blended with relief among the forces at Taji. I felt it. I was exhilarated that the enemy had been eliminated. That was the closest that death had come to our portion of the FOB, but it didn't impact us.

And then I thought about Jesus' admonition to "love your enemies." This was the first time in my life that this passage confronted me in a very real way. His words unavoidably hung there. I felt shame. I also felt anger about Jesus for the shame. If ISIS had existed during Christ's time, would he have thought differently? I didn't know, but I suspected Jesus would still be Jesus in front of ISIS. I just wanted to go home.

But then I wondered: Is that longing for home a longing for self-preservation? Is that feeling an exercise in avoidance? Is it possible to preach the love of God if I cannot explore how that love manifests itself in the darkest places within our world and subsequently our hearts? Is that satisfaction I celebrate in my enemies' death an indictment of my faith? These questions made me uncomfortable because they were necessary and because I had no answer. In my head, I heard songs of fear. Yet, in my heart, I felt my soul speak: "God's mercy falls on the just and the unjust."

But the fear spoke louder.

* * *

Back on the tarmac with the dog in Baghdad, the signal was given by the airman, and we shuffled out to the Chinook. We stayed in line, mindful of the rotor wash and the supplies being loaded. We knew the routine. Load to the front. Watch your legs so that the crew can move up and down the aisle.

I lagged. I had just wanted to pet the dog, but the handler looked at me like I was a pariah. I wanted something pure and unconditional to convince me that this wasn't the real world, but the deployment brought me back into that moment. The only illusions were the ones I was trying to create. I was one of the last loaded onto the helicopter.

The large back portal remained open as we lifted. I had only flown once with the back door completely shut. Then, as on this night, one of the flight crew had sat with his legs dangling off the back of the platform out into the night.

Cautiously, I let my eyes drift to where his seemed to be searching. There didn't seem to be any threat, or at least he didn't seem to be alarmed. Take away the gear and he would have looked like a kid looking out on the Baghdad skyline at night. There was a certain romanticism to the moment.

I looked out over the lights, the buildings, and the trees. It was beautiful. The city was a wandering dialogue of the ancient muddled with the modern. Soft lights illuminated beautiful mosques and narrow streets. There was a playful glow of a large, multicolored Ferris wheel. A driving breeze danced with the date trees. At least at night, all the pockmarks of war had gone to bed in this part of Iraq.

I wondered how long this place would be at war. I wondered, too, how long it would be before I could come back not as an actor of war, but as an admirer of beauty, poetry, and a future filled with hope. I said a silent prayer to the soothing rhythm of the helicopter. I prayed that God showed our enemies a peace in death that had eluded them in life, one that was pure and unconditional. I prayed that I might understand the same and that I might be able to bring that back to the home for which I longed.

The pilot skillfully placed us on the runway on Taji within fifteen minutes.

"Damn, Chap. You still lost in all those thoughts," the soldier said. It was a statement and not a question.

"Always."

I had to think: Years and years of perpetual war in the name of peace left me wondering if maybe we weren't all a little bit lost. I mean, isn't that what happens to us when we can't understand love? We become lost to ourselves and to the grace trying to redeem both us ... and our enemies.

Chapter 7

The Friendships We Forge:
Our Band of Brothers

In 2015, I stood staring at a disheveled mess in my Army office in Tucson, Arizona. All of my nerves twitched at the haphazardness. This space that I used in the Reserve center a host of other people shared with me over the course of the year. Clearly, the individual who had been using it the last month was a proponent of organized chaos, though I was failing to discern any organization.

I didn't feel like cleaning it up. Not this time. This was going to be my last drill—the time the unit gets together for one weekend a month before officially being cross-leveled into the new unit as part of the deployment process. I was still wrapping my mind around it all.

As I picked through a couple of drawers, I heard a knock on the door behind me. I turned to find an unfamiliar enlisted face.

"Sir, do you have a moment?" he asked hesitantly.

"Of course. I don't believe we've met before," I said, extending my hand.

"Actually, sir, we met last month." And I immediately felt like a heel. "I'm a truck driver."

I still couldn't place him, but it didn't really matter. I'm horrible with names (which is why I love the name tape on the uniform), but I'm excellent with faces.

"Come in and take a seat." I closed the door behind him. "I'm sorry the room looks like trash. I'm trying to decide if I am still going to pray for the soldier that left all this mess."

His eyes widened. Sometimes my humor misfires.

"What brings you in here?"

"Well, sir, I just came off active duty ..."

For the next thirty minutes, I participated in the same conversation that I have had with hundreds of new Reserve soldiers over the years. If the soldier had been enlisted, the template was this: Soldier is struggling with marriage due to deployments and operational tempo. Soldier's spouse issues an ultimatum: active duty or me. Soldier comes off active duty, but still wants to serve, and so soldier joins the Reserves. Soldier learns that the civilian world is completely different, often more difficult than life on the active side, and that it's harder to find and maintain a job. Soldier also learns that life in the Reserves is almost antithetical to their time on the active side since structure, discipline, and purpose are harder to achieve on the Reserve side of the house. Within weeks, they resent their spouse, family, new job, and the new unit. If the soldier is an officer, the template is basically identical, but the reason for coming off active duty usually stems from a struggle to be promoted.

This particular conversation was increasingly forlorn because of what weighed on the soldier the most.

"Sir, I miss my friends, and I don't know how to make friends in the civilian world." His eyes welled, but there were no tears.

I didn't know what to tell this guy. I didn't want to be a cliché and tell him to join a club or something.

"I'm sorry." It was all I could think of to say.

Over and over again, especially in my congregational setting, I have encountered men and women who struggled to find adult friendship. I have witnessed this professionally through countless counseling sessions on the deep and pervasive loneliness among adults. I have experienced this personally too.

As a minister, it is difficult to make friendships. The role complicates relationships. We learned in seminary that in order to forge and protect boundaries, we needed to make peace with the fact that we were ministers at all times and in all places. This instruction sought to keep us from blurring boundaries or manipulating power roles within relationships. I understood it then and I understand it now, but I also know that it has created a great deal of emotional isolation in my life.

Like many ministers, I often waited many weeks before I told a new acquaintance what I did as a profession. Once I disclosed the reality of my life, I could typically tell within a few minutes whether this would be the last time we hung out. If they became self-conscious of their speech, especially their use of profanity, or if they immediately started telling me their problems, then I knew that there wouldn't be a friendship. It could be depressing. I could testify to it. This wasn't hyperbole.

I remembered reading an essay by Stephanie Paulsell. If I remember it correctly, she essentially said that being a minister was being the loneliest person in a room full of people. These words have haunted me for years.

When I read the gospels, I wondered about Christ's relationship with the disciples. Were they his friends? Talk about a power imbalance within a relationship! Did Jesus even need friends? I believe he did. God said early in Genesis that it was not good for man to be alone, and so humanity was created. I have to believe that the full humanity of Christ's nature needed friendship, but I suspected from reading the concluding moments of the gospels, especially the moment on Mount Gethsemane, that Jesus was lonely.

I reference this story because it touches on one of the most powerful opportunities a deployment provides—at least, it did for me.

Not long after returning from Iraq, Emily asked me what I missed the most about the deployment.

Without hesitation, I told her, "I miss having friends. I miss the Chief and the Chap."

A huge smile crossed my face.

"Have I told you yet the story of when Chief and I smuggled a pig and cow into an abandoned freezer?

"Um, what?!"

My friendship with Chief was a blessing in the truest sense of the word. I often preached that blessings were moments of grace that defied our capacity for understanding. It's almost like we weren't supposed to understand that grace, just welcome and celebrate it. I don't know why Chief and I were able to hit it off and steadily become great friends, but I stopped overthinking it early on.

Chief was a patriot. He loved his family. He valued the lessons of his West Virginia upbringing. He was hardworking and a team player. He made those around him better at their jobs. He was fair. He had integrity. He was quietly funny. He was industrious and could take surplus materials and craft furniture that will probably outlive Camp Taji. He was respected among his peers, and he was revered among his subordinates. He was better at ping-pong than me, which hurt my pride and church street cred. He was always ready for a cigar and a conversation that gave us a respite from our positions. His flattop and mustache were legendary. I honestly figure that when Americans thank men and women for their service, it is because they imagine people like Chief.

As in all things, there was a certain irony to our friendship. In the civilian world, I doubt we would have become friends. Specifically, I doubt we would have had the opportunity to become friends. Our civilian worlds wouldn't have overlapped enough.

On deployment, our worlds converged regularly. As chaplain I have an embedded role within a very diverse organization, but we all share a common purpose. A chaplain is an officer, but not a normal one. I don't have a defined lane which sets boundaries on my role. It's a challenge, and I was reminded of what a senior chaplain once told me: "You are to be among them, but not of them."

I am unique as an officer in several ways. For example, I can foster conversations and relationships up and down the rank structures of officers and enlisted. Normally, officers can only consort with other officers, and enlisted are constrained to other enlisted. Additionally, there are boundaries between field-grade officers (major to colonel) and company-grade officers (lieutenant to captain). There are similar barriers between noncommissioned officers and junior enlisted ones (private to specialist). Rank enforces these roles. To blur these boundaries is inadvisable and prohibited under the regulations that govern fraternization.

Additionally, I can cross the lanes that exist between job sections. There are administrative, military intelligence, operational, supply, and tech/communication lanes. Over and over, I heard prohibitions against drifting into another section's lane. Those rules didn't typically govern my position. I meet a soldier at the point of their humanity first, not their job.

It sometimes surprised other soldiers to see me exist in such a way.

"How can you talk to that person?" The soldier was peeved. "He is such a terrible soldier."

"Oh. I have no doubt you are right. I've seen him at work. He's probably the worst fork truck driver I've ever seen, and that's only when he shows up on time ... But he's also an amazing husband, a creative thinker, and an articulate soul."

Because of this role and flexibility, I met and befriended Chief. He knew I was a chaplain from the beginning, but this was overcome with our shared purpose and overlapping lives. It was a blessing, for sure.

I was fortunate to serve in a military unit that was filled with real characters. I loved them even when I disliked them. Probably this was a reality in other places and units too, but it was unmistakably true with us. As a general trend, I noticed that the Reserve and Guard side of the house were filled with characters more than the more homogenous active duty soldiers.

Being so intensely immersed in the military world deconstructed an embedded myth I hadn't realized I carried with me about military men and women. Not all soldiers were nice people. Not all soldiers represented the best of America. Some were toxic. Some were abusive. Some were self-serving. I thought we needed to be a little more self-aware about how we lionized the American military. Part of me thought the public was so willing to do this because it helped alleviate the guilt we carry about how these wars have no apparent end in sight.

＊ ＊ ＊

"I can't believe I haven't told you about the huge barbecue that Chief and I pulled off," I told my wife in disbelief.

She stared at me. I think she was weary of stories.

"Well, one of the Geek Squad kids was on assignment in Baghdad ..."

"Wait, wait, who?"

Emily could never remember all the names of the people in my unit, so I created nicknames along the way based on small details that she seemed to remember from previous stories. Some of them stuck. Most of them didn't. I remembered some of them. I forgot most of them. Some were scratched in the margins of my journal. Others I recalled using only once or twice. Some I created during the deployment, some after our return as my memories of friends took on novel qualities. I lamented that some of these nicknames didn't come to me sooner because many of these soldiers would have loved it if I'd called them these names in the country. I added rank on the front to distinguish between officer and enlisted.

For example, here are some of the common characters and friends within the stories I told:

Lieutenant Pretty Kitty Man Boy: He was wonderful, a great friend to many; he was strangely obsessed with cats and would purr intermittently during meetings; he was dedicated to the mission and excitable.

Captain Roomie: He was a proud father and great guy; he was incredibly smart and learned things quickly; he was a former marine even though he hated it when I called him a former marine, since a marine is always a marine; he watched cartoons every morning and played video games every night.

Captain Twins: He was a father to delightful twins; he was experienced in multiple roles over multiple deployments; he was a bit of an asshole, but if you were on his team, he was enjoyable; he reminded me of an insensitive seventy-five-year-old man from a different era, but he had the most tender heart once his twin daughters were mentioned.

Specialists Mafia: These specialists comprised the administrative section; they were diligent and were helpful with the mail; we commonly believed that they sabotaged their own machine so that other units wouldn't require anything of them.

Geek Squad Guys: These specialists were the technical backbone of the unit; they always volunteered to take the hard missions, especially since it got them out of the office and away from the to-do list of Captain Roomie; once, one of them fell from the ceiling, and the chaplain created many stories to explain why it had happened.

Major Ka-Bar/XO: He had a brilliant mind and was a careful listener; he terrified me at first because of a story he told involving his slightly morbid obsession with Ka-Bars, which are extremely large knives; he took directions well, and he executed a mission, which was often tough with the collection of personalities we had; he bought an Iraqi dinner for every section over the course of the deployment.

BC: He was another brilliant mind whose organizational prowess was unmatched; he led with integrity and hard work; he listened; he had a weird habit of eating cucumbers and ice cream for dinner; he loved his family dearly.

So, I continued by sharing the story with Emily about the famous Chief and the Chap Barbecue Rib and Hamburger picnic.

We knew we had personnel assets in Baghdad. We also knew there was a nightly helicopter that came into Taji several times from there. We needed a barbecue smoker, and we needed meat.

If I remember correctly, Chief made friends with some Aussie welders who were fascinated by his knowledge of all things welding and his ability to create Amish-quality furniture. The welders were a bit of a wild card group and kind of kept to themselves except for the few people they let into their world, like Chief. They wanted to do a barbecue for their crew but they didn't have any meat. Chief convinced them to make us a basic smoker in exchange for a bunch of ribs. They jumped at the opportunity. I remember telling the story later that night in the CHU.

"I don't understand." Captain Roomie almost seemed agitated. "How in the hell did you get the Exchange lady to put a special order in for you?" Taji had a Department of Defense- licensed corner store we called the Exchange, which stocked the bare essentials.

"Because we are friends," I responded as if it should have been obvious.

"How?"

"What do you mean, how?" Now I was confused. "Are you asking how I made friends with someone?" He gave me this pained look. "It's easy. I just wasn't a rude to her." I chortled.

"I'm a nice guy too!" He was demonstrative on this point.

"Look, I'm your chaplain and roommate. I like you. Really, I do. But you are an ass."

"Thanks, Chap," he stated genuinely touched.

Somehow one of the contractors on Taji had an extra-deep chest freezer. The contractor and his friends had beautiful voices and sang traditional Fijian gospel songs. I don't know whether the freezer was theirs or why they had delivered it to the chapel, but the chapel was being renovated, so members of the Specialist Mafia moved it to the TOC.

After a month or so, all the planets aligned. The meat was in Baghdad. It was something like twenty racks of ribs and thirty pounds of ground beef. We already had the spices because Chief was Chief and he just magically carried meat rubs and spices with him. Nearly the same day, the smoker was delivered, and Chief was able to source some wood because Chief was Chief.

On a night on which members of the Geek Squad were to make a delivery for computers, we arranged for them to bring back the frozen meat. Everything was going according to plan. Later that night, we met the Specialist Mafia back at the flight line to help them bring the food to the freezer.

We heard the helicopter land from the PAX terminal. We watched as two soldiers comically tried to push a moving dolly filled with boxes the Exchange had given them. Right as they were coming into the PAX terminal, the boxes burst and ten frozen pigs and a fourth of a frozen cow went sliding all over the terminal. The soldiers' eyes got huge, but our laughs were bigger.

Later that week, Chief and I woke up before sunrise to prepare the meats. We laughed and told stories as we seasoned everything. Lieutenant Pretty Kitty Man Boy helped. At the end of the day, Chief and I paused to look at the picnic we had created in the middle of Iraq. There were soldiers from almost all the coalition forces who'd helped us secure stuff. There was the usual cast of characters taking a break to enjoy each other. There were cornhole games and cards. There were friends deepening their friendships.

It was beautiful. It could never have happened in the civilian world.

As I told the story to Emily, my eyes welled a little, but I didn't cry. I knew exactly why that soldier had knocked on my door all those months ago.

I heard a small and hopeful voice within me say, *I miss my friends*. There was an internal pause, and the voiced quivered: *I don't know how to make them anymore.*

And then I heard another voice within me. It was the voice of my calling. All it could say was *I'm sorry.*

Chapter 8

The Stigma of the Army Reserve: You Are Just a Reservist

The Blackhawk bent around the sprawling city below. As the helicopter tipped slightly on its axis, I could see through the open door the outskirts of the city. The land was lush from the streams and canals that wound through the fields and between the homes. Off on the horizon, the Tigris River announced the water's way through these ancient lands.

"By the rivers of Babylon we sat and wept when we remembered Zion," the psalmist had written by the banks of this body of water over which we now drifted. For miles along these shores were rows and rows of date tree plantations. Their branches mirrored the waves upon the waters.

As I glanced at my watch, I released any anxiety. We would be landing in Taji in a few more minutes, so I looked back out to commit to memory the landscapes below us. This moment was a gift. The opportunity to fly by day was a rarity. Normally we moved at night since the enemy did not have the ability to disrupt our movement. On this special day, a general just happened to be doing a "turn and burn" (when an individual makes a quick trip out to a destination and returns the same day) in Besmaya, the Spanish FOB where my religious support team and I had been the last few days providing support to the small footprint of US forces there. A member of the General's entourage had invited us back to Taji on one of the auxiliary helicopters that accompanied the staff everywhere.

I loved ministering in Besmaya. The Spanish were hospitable. They set an unhurried pace. Breakfast was served later than American standards. There was a café break midmorning and then lunch in the early afternoon, at which time the operational tempo slowed for all to rest before a late dinner. As the sun began to set, I would look out and watch the Spanish forces strolling the grounds deep in conversation. I typically returned from this outpost renewed.

The helicopter nestled on the sun-bleached asphalt. I looked at my watch again. I had plenty of time before meeting up with the new division chaplain charged with religious support in Iraq. I was set to give him a tour of the new Resiliency Center that I had led the creation of for Taji.

This achievement merged into one building a cooperative effort between the chaplaincy, the behavioral health professionals, and the civil rights/sexual harassment and assault teams on Taji. Getting these groups to work together was a monumental task. It required walking the building project through its concept phase into construction renderings within the Army's ways and means system located in the US Embassy in Baghdad. The main reason for the project's complexity was simple: each merging group represented a different corps within the Army (chaplain, medical, and JAG—the Judge Advocate General's Corps) and our effort muddied lanes and funding sources. In my mind, however, our partnership kept soldiers from falling through the cracks, which trumped all other concerns about building ownership, program management, and credit for success.

The drive from the PAX terminal to our CHUs was ethereal. I felt as if I existed in a dream or a prayer uttered by one of God's children long ago. I could sense the weight of the deployment's momentum starting to diminish as our days in the country neared an end. This was the last time we were to travel to Besmaya. There might only be one more movement before we began the process of coming home. Once or twice each month of this deployment, my team and I had caught a helicopter or a plane to a distant outpost in order to support a small logistics team that our battalion had sent out.

I chuckled to myself as I thought of the story of how all this had become my job. I drifted into my memories.

"What's with the quail?" the soldier tasked with loading our tough boxes had asked, referencing an image on my box resting in the gravel parking lot of the Reserve Center.

"It's a promise from God," I replied.

The soldier was confused.

"It was a sign from above that God's children would not be forgotten and lost in the desert." I continued, "The story comes from the book of Exodus when the Israelites were convinced that they were going to starve to death in the desert wilderness. The Bible says that God covered the ground in quail so that they could eat. It's the tangible answer to a promise."

I watched my personal effects being loaded into the shipping container. "I feel like I might need that kind of reminder over there."

A quail was a special omen for me. During a difficult season of life, I had contemplated leaving the ministry. I knew that I had been called at the beginning of this journey, but I was wondering whether God still needed me. I fought with it. I questioned it. I felt spiritually arid, and so I prayed through the scriptures of the Exodus.

One morning, while I was reading the passage about the manna and the quail, a family of quail appeared on my fencerow. Each day they returned. In fact, those quail visited us almost every day that we lived in that home during that season of life. I actually had a quail tattooed on my chest in honor of them.

As I turned from the shipping container, another officer asked, "You think you're ready now?"

"Are you kidding me? We have no idea where we're going or what we'll be doing."

He laughed too. "True."

"But I guess I am ready." I thought about it some more. "I mean … It might be a nice break not to be in charge of a church, the programming, and a huge building project."

I thought about our family's impending kitchen construction.

"Besides, what a relief it will be to have only one job for a while."

I turned and left.

Fast-forward two months and a changed mission into Iraq.

"Chaplain Chandler, the division chaplain for Iraq wants you to call him," the battalion commander ordered. He seemed agitated, but continued, "Now listen, I already told him that you were my chaplain and that we needed you for our mission, but I had to consent to his need and Taji's need too."

"Sir, I am not tracking."

"Basically, they don't have any other chaplains on Taji. There's one out on the airfield, but that is pretty detached from the main post, and there are evidently reasons he has to stay out there." He jotted down a quick note. I couldn't imagine all the balls he was trying to juggle right then.

"So ..." I tried to bring him back into the moment.

"You are going to be the chaplain for Taji and run the chapel there. *But*—and I made this clear with him—I still expect that you will travel to our FLEs [small logistics teams] around Iraq, check on our guys, and give me the pulse of our team."

I didn't even really know what to say, but I asked, "Sir, how many people are on Taji?"

"Between all the task forces [coalition military and US military] and contractors, I think we are sitting at about twenty-five hundred."

"Sir, and how many FLEs are we talking about?"

"We are looking at four, but the division chaplain also mentioned a Spanish FOB with a few US troops there that you would need to cover. I am imagining that you will get out once or twice a month to see as many as you can."

"Roger that. I'll do my best."

As I walked down the dirt-encrusted hallways of our new TOC in Taji, I took with me the note with the division chaplain's number on it. I found a phone, dialed the number, and waited.

As the voice of the chaplain answered, I introduced myself.

"Yes, Chaplain Chandler ... I just got done talking to your BC, and I know the expectations he has for you as well," he stated. I would later discover that the conversation between my BC and the division chaplain had been a terse and stern one in the middle of the mess hall.

"That's what I understand, sir," I replied, knowing that a division chaplain is a lieutenant colonel.

"I'll be brief, and we can talk more when I am back in that area later in the week." I could hear him gather some notes.

"I need you to be the Camp Taji chaplain for the installation. This means regular services at the chapel, counseling for the post, and whatever other religious programming you can create. There is another chaplain there, active duty, but he's way out on the airfield. There are too many logistical challenges. He understands that, so there shouldn't be any issues. But he's Unitarian Universalist, which limits the things he can perform, so maybe he can help cover something from time to time. I understand you are the senior pastor of a congregation and can perform general Protestant services, correct?"

"Yes, sir," I answered.

"Additionally, I need you to fly out once a month to a Spanish FOB, Besmaya. There is a small US footprint there, but the chaplain there is Spanish and Catholic. I'll need you to take care of that crew too. Okay?"

"Yes, sir," I answered again.

"One last thing. About one rotation ago, a chaplain from Tenth Mountain created an idea for a chapel expansion project. You will find it in the office. I need you to see if you can get this Spiritual MWR built. Are you tracking?"

A building project. A chapel overseer. A minister to twenty-five hundred personnel. A traveling support barometer. Goodness gracious.

"I'm tracking, but I will have questions when I see you so that I can understand the fullness of your intent." And then I hung up. My chest itched next to my dog tags. I looked down. My quail tattoo was staring right back at me.

I didn't understand why the other units, especially the US ones, didn't have chaplains. Back in Kuwait, Chief joked that he couldn't walk a hundred feet without running into a chaplain. I agreed. I hadn't seen so many in one place since I left the chaplain school at Fort Jackson.

The answer to why other units didn't have chaplains, I learned, involved the "BOG cap"—the number of permanent-party, US military boots on the ground. It was capped at five thousand for all of Iraq. The different task forces were issued only so many spots for soldiers. The second-order effect of this reality was that units would only take mission-essential soldiers into Iraq. Understandably, the units preferred trigger pullers over special staff positions like mine, as well as over social workers, JAG, and specialty doctors. The expectations for this war in Iraq hadn't changed much since the mid-2000s, but we were expected to do it all with less. This also meant that I would have to write three weekly reports— to the battalion, the brigade in Kuwait, and the division in Iraq.

I also learned, eventually, that the active duty chaplain wasn't cool with a reservist being given such a huge task instead of him. At first things seemed positive, and it appeared that a healthy working relationship was possible. I even wondered whether we were going to be able to create a template to overcome the standard friction that exists between the active and Reserve/Guard split.

The broken stereotype played out like this: Reservist/Guard soldiers thought the active all considered themselves better than everyone else. Active soldiers thought the Reserve/Guard soldiers were all junk soldiers, like an island of misfit toys. Both sides carried a chip on their shoulders when interacting with the other side. The Army likes to trumpet, "One team, one fight," but that unity breaks down quickly on component lines.

With respect to the logistics mission in Iraq during Operation Inherent Resolve, I observed that the Reserve/Guard units regularly outperformed the active units. I think we did better because in a mission where we were chronically undermanned and our machines never worked, we were accustomed to that context. Personnel shortages, degrading equipment, and process creativity were the very definition of being in the Reserves. We knew we had to make things work. We were practiced at the creativity necessary to perform within a broken system. For example, I regularly helped carry parts and computers around Iraq on my visits, since the shipping channels were often delayed.

The relationship I forged with the active duty chaplain broke down after a couple of months. I remember coming back from a prolonged trip within Anbar province to find him stewing. He called a meeting between a visiting chaplain and me.

As clear as he was loud, he made it known: "I am the active duty chaplain. I should have been named post chaplain."

The next hour was filled on both sides with puffed chests, bruised egos, and words that could not be unsaid. He glared at me. I don't think he realized how much hate was in his eyes.

"You are just a reservist." One team, one fight? Our working relationship ended right there. I didn't know what glory he thought I was keeping him from achieving.

A typical day in Taji was busy but fulfilling. Being a deployed combat chaplain felt like the best job I have ever had. Though each day was different, there was a driving rhythm that placed me in the lives of hundreds of military and contracted men and women every day. I began with physical training at about 0500 hours. I would talk or work out with whomever was around at that hour. Afterward, I would spend time in devotional study and journaling. I found it ironic that my most disciplined era of prayer and study was in the middle of Iraq. I had struggled to find time for these activities in the States, but in a combat zone they became a natural part of my day. During this time, I would read a psalm and some other text from the Hebrew Bible, and something from the New Testament. I often made a note of the scripture if it spoke to me, adding commentary too. I would then meditate on the scripture as I considered the needs and direction God was placing on me for the day.

Then I would grab a to-go breakfast of pancakes, turkey sausage, and eggs from the DFAC and head to the chapel to open it up in case someone wanted to come early for prayer or to connect with family; our facility had the fastest Wi-Fi signal on post, so it was a popular spot for connecting with home. I would then leave the chapel open with fresh coffee brewing, clean myself up, and head to the daily battle update brief, where I would offer the thought for the day. I usually spent the rest of the morning walking the post and checking in with those I met along the way. I met up with Chief for lunch, but then I would leave early so that I could attend the post base support meetings.

I read and rested in the early afternoon. In the late afternoon, I went back to the battalion to do administrative stuff, check on the FLEs, and to spend time with our team. After dinner, I typically organized some type of event at the chapel like Bible study or music practice. To end the day, I went back to the CHU, read, smoked, or met up with Chief somewhere. Along the way, there were cigar nights, occasional special screenings of movies, and USO (United Service Organizations) events.

When I didn't travel, the life of the chapel was fascinating. I helped shape different types of religious services. In addition to the contemporary Protestant service at which I preached, the chapel hosted a gospel service and a traditional Christian service for a while. My only rules for starting a new Christian Protestant service was that it had to be an hour long (no longer) and that there had to be Communion. We held space for a group of Latter-day Saints soldiers, a Buddhist soldier, and some Wiccan soldiers. Regularly there were visiting Catholic chaplains to offer Mass, and we hosted coalition chaplains visiting their soldiers. There was an Australian padre who offered many beautiful events.

I was constantly astonished by the gifts and talents of soldiers who intersected in the life of the chapel. There were soldiers whose musical ability often brought tears to my eyes, or ones who would offer prayers and testimonials during the service that would rival any great sermon. I remember the first time I led the chapel during a rotation of units. I was nervous about losing some of the lay leaders who had really created something beautiful in this worship space in Iraq. Each time one group moved on, God always provided new leaders and new talents. It was a powerful lesson in trust. I was frequently touched by the faith of others and the vulnerability that they showed so courageously on a weekly basis.

The chapel also provided some unintentional blessings that would shape my ministry in Taji. Because we had such good Wi-Fi, I ensured that we had the best coffee on post, too. Over the course of the deployment, hundreds of people sent me coffee upon request. Their gifts created a spot for true hospitality. The chapel became an intersection of community as interpreters, many from Iraq, Syria, and Afghanistan, sat with coalition forces and discussed the things that make us human, like family, faith, love, and hope. That surely was what the true community in the New Testament looks like.

I loved the interpreters. They were mostly older and had witnessed multiple wars over multiple years around the Middle East. Regularly, they uttered the phrase *en shala*, which roughly translates to "in God's timing." The joke among the coalition forces was that this phrase really meant "I will get to it when I get to it. Have some coffee." I found the phrase to be perfect for this group. To be sure, they were slow-moving people. One interpreter said, "We operate out of an ancient perspective. We see ourselves as a very small slice of an ancient story." Why rush, then? This attitude created a struggle to motivate interpreters based on Western deadlines. I grew to think that they added an essential perspective on the pace of war. Thank God for strong coffee and fast Wi-Fi.

The chapel was a place of connection and sabbath for the personnel at Taji. It was also a place of those virtues for me too. On Monday afternoons, I was able to steal away to the chapel to watch movies and read with absolutely no one else around me. During my deployment I read some of the best books of my life. I immersed myself in the world of Harry Potter for the first time, and in *Lonesome Dove*. I relished this time—of not being needed for a spell. The chapel became a special place for my family too. Every Sunday night, after services but before my own family headed to church on Sunday morning back in the States, we would share Communion over video chat. Over the course of the deployment, my children learned the Words of Institution as well as the Lord's Prayer. Those times of Communion kept me centered eternally within their love. I was so grateful.

And then there were the travel weeks, which were crazy. I could try to map out a game plan, but movement throughout Iraq was unpredictable. I created a plan of action based on locations that were of value to the command team or that we had not been to in a while. Most of the distant FOBs had at least one religious support team, but because our FLEs were so small and easily overlooked by the FOB leadership structures, our battalion commander was sensitive to the welfare and morale of these soldiers. Routinely, a soldier situation would occur at one of the FLEs and I would be deployed to help.

There were several common problems with such travel. First, it was nearly impossible to forecast when I could return to Taji because flights out of the FOB were inconsistent. One particular plane was infamous for being delayed or canceled: Chrome 50. The places we went were austere with active live fire out to enemy positions. It was common to get stuck at a location for up to ten days, which made covering the chapel a challenge in our absences. Luckily, a Guard unit placed a chaplain on Taji to help with the occasional needs around the chapel. Unfortunately, the first one they sent had to redeploy due to health issues, but the chaplain that replaced him was phenomenal. To this day, I remain friends with her. Another common issue with travel was sleeping in the transient tents. These were special bays of cots that gave you a place to crash and store your stuff. But the tents were rarely cleaned and so were disgusting. They smelled. They were often sticky and crusty.

Last, I just never knew what I was walking into with these FLEs. On average, these were worthwhile trips since some of the FLEs were hot messes. Others thought I was a spy for the BC and so they were standoffish. Still others just did not want the responsibility of having visitors. One way or another, I always found those visits fascinating. And then one night the stars and winds would align, and we'd make it safely back to Taji in the middle of the night.

Slowly but surely with each passing week, what started as a concept in cooperation—the Resiliency Center—came into being with the help of many, many people, but most especially that of a lieutenant from the Nevada National Guard. She had an innate ability to understand the people behind the Army process. When the time came to cut the ribbon, I felt disingenuous holding the scissors by myself, especially since she was the one who had found someone to make the scissors! She typified the genius often unexpectedly found in the Guard and the Reserves.

I was proud of all that was achieved with the opening of that center and all the other daily ways I was able to make an impact, even if only as a reservist. I repeatedly got asked, "How did you have the energy? You must have drawn it from your faith."

I would like to think the truest parts of my motivation came from my love of God and sense of call, but I know it was also driven by ego and anxiety, an embedded need to overachieve and not disappoint. All the same, when the deployment neared an end and I received a Bronze Star, it was humbling, but also a confirmation that I really had worked hard under challenging conditions with multiple job descriptions, including one that perpetually put me in vulnerable situations and one that was normally held by someone of a much higher rank.

"You don't get a Bronze Star just for doing your job well?" I was asked right after I got home. I know he wasn't trying to be disparaging, but it stung. I wondered how many burning buildings I needed to escape or how many confirmed kills I needed on my record before I earned such a medal.

"Sort of," I replied.

The Bronze Star, in general, created controversy. Many soldiers felt that it was awarded too liberally. I was somewhat sympathetic to their arguments. I am sure it is completely possible that too many of these have been handed out over the years, but I didn't care. I was a captain who went above and beyond what is normally asked of a battalion chaplain, to the point that I also performed as a major by providing support to an entire post, and to the level of a lieutenant colonel by reimagining a failed blueprint and turning it into the Resiliency Center. I circulated through a battle space at war, ran a post chapel with robust programming, and forged corps-level partnerships.

I was proud of my Bronze Star. I ended the conversation.

The ride from the PAX terminal to my CHU ended, and I met my new boss for the last two months of my deployment. The new division chaplain and I were wrapping up the tour. He replaced the one who'd initially gave me the assignment. I reminded myself to thank the new chaplain assistants who had helped clean the space. Every room smelled of lemon-pine-inspired chemicals.

"How did you get this all done?" he asked as he flipped through the literature sitting out.

"Sir, I am just a reservist." I tried to say it as ironically as possible.

He let out a nervous laugh.

"I am used to having two jobs plus family. Building the Resiliency Center was easier than trying to potty train my kids! I guess I was looking for something to do in all my free time."

He let out a real laugh this time.

"Honestly, sir, the hardest part of this project was fighting over the name with the general!" We walked down the long hall outside the chapel as we headed from the office suite where the behavioral health, civil rights, and sexual harassment and assault offices were located.

"You see, sir, I had a great series of names picked out. I even created storyboards for them so that the general could see it." I turned to him. He had a smile on his face.

"Every time I pitched a new name, the general would respond, 'I love it! The Resiliency Center.' I would try to correct him and give him a new name, but he responded the same: 'Perfect! The Resiliency Center.' So, I just threw away the storyboards. I hope you liked your tour of the Resiliency Center!"

He laughed and laughed.

Later that night, I headed back to my CHU. It was a solitary place. A special mission up north near Mosul had taken my roommate away for the week. I crashed on my bed, but I'd forgotten that I needed a new journal since I'd finished another during the trip to Besmaya.

I went over to my tough box. The image of a quail greeted me. I pulled out a clean journal. At that moment, a prayer formed from my lips onto the pages, there by the rivers of Babylon as I dreamt of home.

Chapter 9

The Struggle with Relationships: A Fight with Loneliness

When Emily and I married years ago, our Texas beach ceremony included the recitation of a familiar portion of Solomon's lyrical letter to his lover: "I am my beloved's and my beloved is mine." When Solomon uttered these sensual words, it was part of a larger longing fueled by the fullness of the spirit. This wasn't a base articulation of an erotic urge. It was a recognition that intimacy, including sexual intimacy, was a gift of the spiritual, the emotional, and the physical. These intimacies are interwoven within the larger blessing of two souls finding meaning and a future together. Emily and I found depth in these declarations, and so Solomon's words capped our vows and sealed our covenant to each other.

I say all this to prepare you for the fact I am a normal person. I require intimacy. At the end of the day, like every living entity, I am a relational being, even a sexual one. Take a deep breath. This might be difficult to read. (And as I said in the author's note early on, you might choose to skip it.) I know this does not come up too often (read *never*) in my communion meditations or the blessings I offer at monthly potlucks. Emily and I do not discuss the intimate nature of our relationship at family gatherings around the holidays. Like most men, I do not brag about the sexual details of my relationship with my wife, nor do I engage in "locker room talk," which does not exist except between sleazebags. At the end of the day, my sacred covenant with my wife is essential to my identity as a man, husband, father, minister, and chaplain. In all ways, I seek to preserve and enrich our relationship and our shared intimacy. It is that simple.

Don't give me sainthood yet. I am human. I am not oblivious to the attractiveness of other women, but like most married men I am able to exercise self-control. Amazingly I can achieve this without instituting silly bans on one-on-one conversations with women. I simply value women.

I know most people prefer to think of ministers as asexual entities. I don't blame them. I don't really fight for them to think differently. Considering that people have reductionist tendencies, I fear being limited and defined by my sex life. I cringe at the thought. I do not want people imagining the happenings of my bedroom while I am up in front of the church preaching. People know that I have engaged in sexual acts at least three times, since I have three children, but that's probably all their minds will let them consider. I figure that I have some parishioners who look at our children and assume that as a servant of God I qualified us for the immaculate conception route of bringing children into the world. I get it. I understand it. Part of me is perfectly fine with their willful ignorance on the matter. As a minister, I live in a glass house. It is fine by me if my bedroom has curtains!

"Then why even bring up this stuff with physical intimacy and sex?" Emily asked uncomfortably as she read these opening paragraphs.

"Because once I pushed past the fear of being there, one of the hardest parts about being in Iraq was the vacuum of intimacy. I missed you. It was terrible. I missed your touch. I missed hugs and kisses. I missed the gentle hand on my back at night ... And I missed all the 'other' things. Celibacy was weird," I stated uncomfortably.

"I get it, but why is it important to the whole story?" She clearly did not like my answer.

"Because most of the counseling and praying I did in Iraq stemmed from the breakdown of intimacy, the blurring of boundaries, the failures of lust-filled decision-making, and the destruction of relationships. And it is too hard to pass judgment on these soldiers unless I am able to unveil to people how soul-crushing it really is, even for a minister of the gospel with an amazing wife and three children." I folded my arms in front of me as I made the point. My grandfather used to do the same when he made his final point.

And then she gave me the look. Tread carefully, her eyes declared.

A combat zone is one of the most intimately arid places I have ever experienced. It is a vacuum of physical intimacy. No one really touches anyone for any reason. I am speaking more broadly than of sexual touch, which is prohibited by regulation. The military is a lot like church camp in that regard: no purpling!

I am referring to things like embraces or gentle punches. I am talking about the normal touching that happens between friends and coworkers. I am talking about the physical contact that most take for granted. In Iraq, there were no hugs—not even side hugs! There were no pats on the back for a job well done, no moments of encouragement. There were no steadying hands on the shoulder of a soldier going through an emotionally wrought moment. There were not even that many handshakes, as saluting is the required courtesy. A soldier can go days and weeks without ever actually touching another human being beyond the accidental contact of confined spaces.

We humans are not at our best in such an environment. Early in our sacred scriptures, we tell a story that God discerned we were not complete without the benefit of another. God reached into creation to bring fullness to humanity. It troubled God that humankind might wither within a solitary existence, so God created a partner and thus the possibility of relationship. God fashioned women and men equally within the image of the holy. The resulting relationship was one constructed on mutuality and love. These two qualities form the basic template between all relationships, including friendships.

Intimacy is crucial to the development, sustenance, and nurturing of relationships. Therefore, on deployment I found it both fascinating and disheartening to witness how critical touch is to intimacy. I spent months trying to understand what overarching value the military sought in creating this type of environment. Considering my caseload of forlorn souls in need of counsel, I could not determine any strategic advantage of a touch-free existence because it seemed to break down the soldiers' humanity, which subsequently broke down their resilience, which then affected the soldiers' effectiveness. An officer's staff cannot function properly if one of the essential cogs in the machine is constantly having to be rebuilt by the chaplain.

It was not until I was back in Tucson post-deployment that I had an insight into why the military might implement such a system. I was speaking at a retired teachers association for Veterans Day. I was commenting on intimacy during war. I shared my thoughts on the matter. Afterward, a gentleman asked if he could have a word with me. We walked to a corner.

With nervous eyes, he scanned the room, while out of the corner of his mouth he said, "It's about distance. Professional distance."

"Excuse me? I am confused," I replied.

"You have to create distance between you and the soldiers underneath you." His eyes locked on mine. "You have to be able to give orders that could potentially lead them to their deaths or to the death of their brothers. That's why there isn't intimacy over there."

There was a pause within that moment. I felt God guide my silence, for this was not my moment to speak.

"It's strange. The relationships you form among your peers in combat are legendary, and yet you have to keep such distance between you and those tasked with carrying out your orders. It's the only way the mission can succeed," he stated with such a heavy burden. His eyes drifted away from me and to his wife making her way over to us. A smile formed on his lips and we parted company.

In the military I learned early and tangibly that there were second- and third-order effects to the decisions, policies, and actions made. The gentleman was correct. Professional distance was indeed necessary in the intense moments that frequently manifested within war. Historically, these have been times when the order was given to charge a position or disarm an IED manufacturer. There are real consequences to these moments which can create physical, emotional, and spiritual consequences that a soldier deals with the rest of their life. I ministered to those consequences every day. And this brings me back to sex.

A dangerous cocktail begins to emerge when one removes the things that enhance our boundaries and protect our humanity. Let's consider the role of touch within intimacy, or more specifically, what happens when touch is no longer part of one's daily existence. It cannot be overstated: When you remove touch, a vacuum forms. Within this vacuum, positive aspects of our creation are replaced with extra helpings of the ingredients adrenaline, aggression, uncertainty, boredom, insecurity, lust, and the dissonance that comes from distance. I mean, really: What could go wrong? Throw in the fact that many of these soldiers are in their early twenties and you begin to see an emerging storm of emotional immaturity and existential pollution. I kept very busy, and it didn't take long.

This vacuum slowly creaked open the doors to loneliness. The darkness ushered it in. I did not know if it was a sign of love or weakness, but I was already pining for Emily after a few short weeks. I would scroll through our pictures with regret that I took for granted the power of her embrace. After a month, I wrote to Emily. I took my first stab at the long military tradition of longing love letters. I wrote as poetically as possible on how much I missed her physical presence in my life and in my arms. I missed the smell of her hair, the warmth of her breath on my chest, and the softness of her body.

I dared not discuss it with anyone, as the rest of the crew appeared unfazed. It did not occur to me that others were struggling with loneliness until an offhand conversation on a stoop in Kuwait. Dinner was over. An older soldier and I were passing time as we waited for others to join up. We were preparing to see our second movie of the day, which was the discussion topic of the moment. As we waited, a group of young women passed by on their way to the gym. In Kuwait, official military uniforms were only required during the working day. After 1700 hours, those at the installation were permitted to wear civilian clothes. Sometimes I wondered if there was a contest that I didn't know about, because after 1700 hours, soldiers—both men and women—would put on clothes that were as tight as clothes could be, seeking to show off their fitness and youth. The passing women were clearly fit and drew the attention of our conversation.

As the women walked past, I heard the soldier exhale in an almost defeated way. "I can't believe that I can't stop looking at them. I've already got desert dick."

I did not know what to say. I had no clue what he was talking about. However, I hoped it was not contagious, as I did not remember that being one of the hundreds of vaccinations we had received before coming over here.

"Holy s---, I miss my wife!" He looked at me and then at my cross. "S---. I'm sorry for cussing, Chaplain."

Soldiers get nervous about profanity in front of the chaplain. It's kind of cute.

"Just pray for me, okay? I wasn't ready to deploy again. We weren't ready for it."

At first listen, one might think this guy was joking, but he was sincere.

The next morning, I cornered one of my new friends at breakfast. Talking in a hushed voice, I quickly scanned the table to make sure I was not being overhead. I asked him what, exactly, was this syndrome the older officer had self-diagnosed. The coffee spilled in his lap. He jumped up as the steam rose from his lap. I laughed. He did not.

"Chaplain, you've got to give me warning. Where did you hear that?"

I told him. He laughed. I did not.

At the beginning of a deployment, there was this game the soldiers like to play: Shock the Chaplain. They think it's humorous to embarrass us. They do this because most chaplains are culturally conservative: They watch only clean movies and abhor profanity. These chaplains try to recreate the evangelical bubbles of their churches. Soldiers love trying to pop this bubble.

A perfect example of this occurred before we left Arizona. We had a special class on what personal items to pack and what types of items would be prohibited. Most of the conversation centered on how soldiers could bring their gaming systems and what types of plugs would be needed to make them work.

From the rear of the room, one of the crusty officers shouted, "What about our Fleshlights?"

I was confused, and I leaned over to the guy next to me.

"I assumed the Army would supply us with flashlights. Do I have to buy one of those too?" I had meant for this comment to only be audible to my neighbor. The class broke out in laughter and turned in my direction.

"Fleshlights, Chaplain! Not flashlights!" the officer roared as the others rolled.

I deplore being the butt of a joke, but I was helpless. I had no idea what a Fleshlight was or why it was apparently hilarious. And then the game began. With great bravado the officer informed me that a Fleshlight was a sex toy for men. All the eyes locked on me. I knew they were trying to see how embarrassed I was. To be clear, I was embarrassed. He had me and he knew he did. Everyone became quiet. I sensed that the object of the game was to embarrass the chaplain, but not humiliate me. I was both.

Back to the breakfast table. As my friend mopped up the coffee, he chuckled. "Desert dick is when you get stuck in a depressing environment, far from your wife or girlfriend, and the girls you normally wouldn't look at twice become objects of obsession."

I considered his words as I sipped my own coffee. The notion seemed depressing if it was legitimate. I already missed my wife, and it had only been a month. My journal was full of simple observations of longing for Emily during these weeks. I could not imagine it getting worse. The look on my friend's face told me that it would get much worse.

"I won't lie to you, Chaplain. It will get tough. In another three weeks, those girls that just walked by will take on mythic qualities, haunt your dreams, and occupy your free time ... if you know what I mean." He stated this matter-of-factly.

"Like goddesses of war?" I asked.

"Yes!" He exclaimed. "That's the perfect way to describe it."

I retreated to my thoughts again. Most of the time I preferred to be right. It was not a spiritual gift, I knew. I did not enjoy being right at this moment.

My friend broke the silence. "That's only half the story." He took a drink from his coffee, "All these dudes' wives and girlfriends are experiencing the same stuff back in the rear, and in the next couple of months the snakes in the grass will start to strike. That's when you learn your best friend is sleeping with your wife or some other type of story. Just wait. The text messages will start to come in, and guys will learn on Facebook that their girlfriend is cheating on them or something like that. You will be busy, Chap!"

I sensed that these words were a premonition of things to come, but I was unprepared for how true they would be in the end. I think that I had a guileless perspective on deployment that most Americans shared. I believed we all thought or hoped that the honor and sacrifices of our servicemen and servicewomen were somehow able to form a protective cocoon around their relationships. I think it was the product of the public's guilt. In some sense, we already feel sorrowful about the reality of war for those who serve on our behalf. It would be too much to think about the strain it places on the soldiers' relationships, and so we willfully turn a blind eye as we wave the American flag to all those that pass by.

"How do most guys handle it?" I asked. I assumed that most wanted to keep their relationships.

"I don't know. I guess each person has their own way, but not many of them are probably healthy," he answered, and then plowed into his food, which had gotten cold.

I took his cue. I did not want to keep this conversation going. I was self-conscious, and I felt so far away from my wife. Looking at the calendar in my mind, counting down the days, grief seeped into this moment. The real fight with loneliness had begun.

I began to consider the nature of relationship, specifically the spiritual union of two souls, their covenant. The idea of covenant was interesting. The word was used in a plurality of ways both inside and outside of the church. I often taught within my faith community that it was a sacred understanding between two parties that was created out of a shared understanding of the holy, which guided the journey between the two. In this way, covenant was often used to describe humanity's relationship with God, or individuals' relationships with Christ and with each other. We use covenantal language for baby dedications, baptisms, and new church members.

Marriage was also defined as a covenant. On the surface, there were these two people physically and emotionally joining together to create a future together. Below, there was a spiritual current organizing and creating a system of roots, which then grounded the relationship in something eternal, something beyond the physical or even the emotional. In my experiences of ministry, when breakdowns of covenant occurred, it was generally due to a neglect or degradation of the spiritual union. The physical and emotional lapses were the symptomatic expressions of that deeper failure.

After ten years of ordained ministry and nine years of marriage, I discovered a blind spot in my understanding and teaching of covenant. Prior to deployment, I'd treated this spiritual union as a one-time ceremony. This was a mistake. Though the covenant may have had a ceremonial beginning, it was not a one-and-done theological moment. Rather, it functioned like an ethic. Covenant requires practice. It demands a daily decision to live into it so that it can continue to grow and develop. Every day that did not begin with this choice was a day in which covenant's development was arrested. One can only go so many days without nourishing this relationship before the covenant begins to break down. Most of us make this decision unconsciously each day when we wake up and go about life with our partner. Deployment changes that calculation. Iraq forces one to make that which was unconscious conscious every single day or face the unwanted consequences.

Sure enough, my friend was prescient. Most soldiers did not handle the vacuum of intimacy and loneliness in healthy ways. In fact, it dramatically exacerbated the effect of poor decision-making. If a soldier woke up and did not make that conscious decision to honor his or her covenant, then they were symbolically (and at times literally) flirting with disaster. The same would be true for the loved ones back in the rear, for the full weight of the deployment is felt by everyone.

When breakdowns in covenant occur, the way they manifest is sometimes predatory, sometimes innocent, sometimes absurd, sometimes planned, sometimes lamented, sometimes celebrated, and almost always inexcusable. I watched helplessly at times. There were coed sports activities like basketball, football, or frisbee that became way too handsy, to the point of professional lines being crossed. There were drifting brushes of body parts as one soldier passed another soldier in confined spaces. There were accidental shared meals that over time became standing dates. There were simple friendships that morphed into "deployment spouse" status as friendships crossed lines into the emotional and then the physical. There were movie nights in CHUs that lasted well beyond the final credits. There were obsessions with the goddess, and there was stalking of the goddesses. There was a proliferation of pornography and self-pleasuring. I cannot count the number of times I stayed on the double bunks in transient tents and tried to fall asleep as all the noises and rhythmic shaking of loneliness filled the space.

About halfway through the deployment, I grew tired of this vacuum of intimacy. Though this reality was the byproduct of war, it did not mean that I could not change it, even if in only a small way. I decided to implement an old church trick: the hug. At Saguaro, I give a hug to every person who wants one. My default is the side hug, but I would go in for the full thing if the situation required it. Experience taught me that for some of our members, a hug can be the only physical contact they experience in a week. The positive impact in moments like this cannot be overstated. At first I did not think the soldiers would be receptive to giving and receiving hugs. They were alphas, tough. I was wrong. Even some of our toughest soldiers would take a hug from the chaplain. As a tool, I cannot quantify its tangible impact other than my intuition said it helped. I would like to think that a simple hug filled a void long enough for some of them to avoid a disastrous decision later that night.

I counseled hundreds of soldiers in Iraq. The majority of those sessions were due to the second- and third-order effects of loneliness within this vacuum of intimacy. These soldiers were pained and lost and longing. Pornography was a readily available outlet. I know pornography elicits strong opinions. It became clear to me that explicit material was a sad escape, a barometer of loneliness, and mostly a shame-filled cancer that drove wedges of separation into relationships and caused many awkward moments between roommates.

There were conversations during which I had to hide my rage as I listened to the victims of predatory advances. I had guessed that it would be the younger enlisted men who would be the main perpetrators of sexual harassment, but it was actually usually the older soldiers, or, as I began to label them, the "one-deployment-too-many guys." It was not always men either. I was surprised by the number of women who engaged in this type of behavior. Then there were the sad conversations. The ones filled with broken hearts. These were situations with soldiers who did not fully realize that they had gone so far with someone other than their partner until they saw it in their partner's eyes when confronted over video messaging after their partner discovered intimate emails.

Managing my own loneliness was a challenge too. I cannot pretend that it was not. But keeping a covenant is a decision one makes every day. Gratefully, I didn't compromise this covenant with infidelity or by creating a deployment spouse. It was the best daily decision I made. And then those days passed, and one day, after a painfully long time, I was reunited with my beloved Emily, and it was transcendent, and it was private. I was my beloved's and my beloved was mine.

Recently, I was able to talk with my friend from Iraq about all of this.

"I'm so glad that I pushed through all of it without ruining my relationship," I told him. "It seemed like we'd never be home when we were there, but now it feels like it went by so fast. I can't imagine what would've happened if I'd succumbed to desert dick."

He spilled his water on his lap. Just like old times. We laughed.

"I forgot about that!"

"Well, I don't think I ever will. Loneliness is one hell of a fight," I said as I handed him a napkin.

"Amen," we both echoed.

A chaplain is one of the few people who can testify to the damage and trauma these wars have caused to the humanity and relationships of millions. I do not believe the American public wants to know the true covenantal cost of these wars. I think they prefer ignorance. It's one of the great tragedies of war.

Chapter 10

The Mistakes Made: Two Failures

Jesus looked at Peter and said, "Before the rooster's crow, you will fail me multiple times."

In the gospel of Luke, Peter's response was, "There's no way."

Peter knew that he and the disciples did not always have everything figured out, but they did have grit. In these pivotal concluding moments of Jesus' journey, Peter bucked the thought that he would fail or that he even could fail.

And then there were the denials. And then the cock crowed.

Failure is a complicated gift. On the one hand, the lessons learned from one's mistakes create opportunities for greater learning, deeper insights, and ultimately a higher performance. This only works, however, if the failure doesn't destroy the person or the path. At Saguaro, we adopted a borrowed mantra, "Fail often to succeed sooner," which we used as a motivator to take risk. I repeatedly turned our church's attention to the disciples as described in the gospels.

"We should find comfort in their cluelessness," I told my leaders. "It's a journey that we don't have to have figured out. We need to be willing to have the courage to go where Christ goes. We will make mistakes, but we will pray that the Spirit shapes those moments into a greater faithfulness."

I've inserted some variation of the above into leadership training sessions, sermons, and newsletter articles over my time at the church. I prayed that these lay leaders would take the chance to do something that reflected the love we encounter in the gospels.

I truly believed that "we can do all things through the Christ that strengthens us," as Paul wrote to a community of faith that was daring to dream big. Honestly, if followers of Christ could not think big, were we even being good stewards of our faith?

This was the philosophy by which I led communities. But it was not how I lived personally. I hated mistakes, especially silly, small ones. I cannot imagine that I was unique as a minister in seldom offering myself the same grace that I willingly bestowed on others. I knew this wasn't fair, but I felt like the most effective leaders were the ones who saved all the margins of error for their people, which meant that the leader needed to be as close to flawless as possible and to embrace a work ethic that covered the gaps that bedevil an institution. I didn't want my failure to destroy Saguaro or end its journey.

I carried this personal and professional philosophy of failure to Iraq as I stepped into a role for which it was impossible to be completely prepared. This approach wasn't helpful. I knew before I left that it wasn't, but I didn't know how else to lead. Often, this approach spawned and then fed off my anxiety. Often, it drove me to work harder—but that took time away from prayer and critical reflection or self-dialogue. Without these last two tools, I inhibited my own ability to evaluate the errors healthily. I absurdly took ownership of gaffes that weren't of my own making. I treated all failure equally even though some of the mistakes were innocently born of inexperience. Every failure took on unrealistic proportions, as if it had the potential end to my career or my marriage or my integrity. I deluded myself that I would always remember these faults and that they would define me irrevocably.

Actually, I don't remember 98 percent of them. And actually, they don't define me. It turned out that all those hair shirts I wore under my uniform were unnecessary.

There were two mistakes, however, that I made which I still remember vividly. These mistakes were failures that were entirely my fault. One occurred from a need to be liked. The second happened due to pure hubris. Both were humbling. Both made me a better human, soldier, and chaplain.

Failure 1: Club Membership Revoked

I failed early in the deployment. It was a carryover of a recurring theme with which other ministers have struggled too, probably since the beginning of ministry. My failure was drawing too many of my social connections and needs from the community I was tasked with serving.

In congregational ministry, relational boundaries are tough, but I had learned the value of peers and access to a community beyond the church. Emily and I had discovered firsthand how devastating it could be if we allowed the church to have too much of a role in our family's life and well-being. When professional and personal boundaries blurred, it was often the personal protections that eroded first. Thus, professional disagreements became acutely personal, and feelings of betrayal were common on all sides. As a retired minister once put it, "You learn to be friendly with everyone, but friends with so very few."

In a deployment, relational boundaries take on an almost mythic level of difficulty, but the need for friendship remains unchanged, if not more pronounced. I figured as much before departing, but I had no frame of reference for how the deployment would be. I was new to the unit and to the theater. Every day was new. It was intense, especially since I am naturally an overachieving people pleaser. There were very few peers on whom I could lean. Chaplain relationships in the military were suspect at best anyway, especially considering I was a progressive chaplain in a predominantly evangelical and fundamentalist Christian milieu. To add insult to injury, there was no community beyond the community I was embedded to serve.

Consider also that my wife, my best friend, was half a world away. She needed to focus on the kids. She needed to focus on herself so that she could make it. How fair would it have been if I had expected her to be in Iraq what she was to me in Tucson? That's not realistic.

My parents were struggling with the weight of the deployment and their health was precarious. If I had shared with them my fears and the things I was thinking, then that would only have worsened their fears. I worried that too much information might literally kill them. I could not do that to them.

The few friends I had were busy people. They had their own churches, their own families, and their own problems. They didn't have a frame of reference for the challenges I faced. They weren't military. I didn't have time to explain every acronym, section, unit, or rank. I didn't have the energy, and neither did they.

Then there was the reality that units stuck to themselves. Infantry hung out with infantry. Reserve didn't mix that much with the Guard, and neither of us got invited to the active table. The different branches kept to themselves. The same was true of the different coalition forces. At least on the surface, the deployed life was stratified and isolated.

Thus, natural relationships tended to forge between individuals within a unit, of kindred rank, and of the same component and country. For me, if we set aside my position, this meant I had a potential built-in social circle of about nine captains and a few lieutenants, or the Captain Club, as I jokingly referred to them in my journal.

But I am the chaplain. Their chaplain. My role was clear even if the boundaries were not. I wasn't just another officer who could fill multiple roles within the unit. I served them alone.

When our unit arrived in Kuwait, we carried with us a brewing situation. There was a looming tension between the Captain Club and the command team, specifically with the CSM (command sergeant major), the senior enlisted soldier and advisor to the battalion commander. There were questions concerning her professional competency, which had crept into the realm of gossip and character assaults. It got ugly.

While in Kuwait, a decision was made that all soldiers minus the command team and two other field-grade officers were to sleep in one transient bay. This meant that officers and enlisted would be sharing the same living space. This also meant that the discord between the captains and the command team parked itself right in the middle of everyone. This living situation was like a tinderbox. Often, this compounded work stress, as leaders had no separation from their subordinates or vice versa. Within a week, the bay reeked of pettiness, conflict, and foot fungus. I wrote in my journal, "Holy moly! It is like I am living in my old middle school!"

Now, I was not immune to all of this. I was tired. I was frustrated by the decision-making. I shared in the bickering. It felt good to feel like I was one of the crew, embracing the suck and participating in that time-honored Army tradition of complaining. I was human, but I forgot that I was also the chaplain. To the enlisted soldiers watching me in these situations, I was just another petulant officer disparaging the enlisted community. To the Captain Club, I was projecting that I was more "*of* them" than merely "*among* them."

The situation continued to deteriorate, to the point that the Captain Club no longer pretended to hide their contempt for the CSM. The situation boiled over the day that the command team arrived at the office and discovered that the CSM's chair had been stolen. To this day, I still don't know who pulled the prank. The XO (executive officer) rightfully exploded. He pulled all the officers into a room and minced no words.

"Pathetic," he snarled.

He was right. But he did not stop there.

As the reprimand was breaking up, I slipped down the hall to speak to the battalion commander. As a chaplain, I had an open door to the commander. I was to use that privilege as a way to assist leadership on matters of morale.

"Sir, you have a problem," I meekly offered.

He glowered.

Though I was an advisor to the commander, I had never tried to have a difficult conversation with this particular battalion commander prior to this moment. I stood before him. Immediately I second-guessed being in that room. I did not know how to diffuse this situation or shape it in a way to set him up for success. I did not know him, either as a person or as a leader.

I gave him an overview of the breakdown occurring within the ranks. I attempted to speak in generalities regarding the captains' perception of the CSM. I tried to apologize for my complicity in perpetuating the situation.

Before I could even finish, he stormed down the hall. I chased after him. The officers were still milling about in the room as the BC entered.

It became clear to me during his lambasting of the officers that I, even as I strived to be vague, evidently had confirmed for him several things that were severely problematic. Because he was standing partway into the room, I found myself stuck behind him as he admonished the officers in front of me, revealing things that I didn't know had been happening. The anger and anguish in the room was palpable. I could see that from over his shoulder as I peered into the room.

To the Captain Club, the optics on this situation were horrible. From their perspective, two minutes after talking with the BC, I was standing behind him nodding my head as he dressed them down for very specific things, some of which I had perpetuated, but clearly he was not treating me as a culprit. To them, I must've looked like a narc. To them, I had betrayed their friendship.

Failures rarely resolve themselves. Typically, they only fester.

That ten-minute series of events has played in my head more times than I care to admit. I had messed up. I was complicit in the whole series of events. I learned from it, however, which made me a better chaplain.

To begin with, I discerned a few best practices particular to this situation. I learned that on my first day I should have discussed with the BC how he wanted me to help him navigate the conflict that frequently results from the inevitable issues which are a part of every unit's life cycle. I should have asked the XO for his ideas and hopes for keeping things contained so that the BC didn't get overwhelmed with shallow problems. I should have asked the CSM how she wanted me to communicate discontent with her, including my own.

I also should have spoken to the command team sooner. I should have lobbied the company commander more quickly for a creative solution to the billeting or housing situation. I should have pulled fellow captains to the side and offered them an appropriate and professional place to vent. I should have found the same place for myself. That was what a solid chaplain operating among the soldiers would have done.

Ultimately, I should have not waited until the chair was stolen. But I wanted friends. I needed to be liked. To the surprise of none, even after apologizing to several of the captains, I was out of the club.

I also took away larger insights into the role of chaplaincy and its relationship to the commander. I learned that advisement is more than just information. It requires relationship and shared understanding of the commander's priorities and expectations. It functions best when there is a clear direction that the chaplain seeks to understand.

Finally, I learned that the role of a chaplain was absolute. Soldiers may entertain me as just one of the crew, but my contributions would always be fundamentally interpreted by the cross I wear on my uniform.

For a while after this event, I wondered whether friendship was possible. I discovered it was, but with a significant amount of intentionality. When Chief and I became friends, he told me over cigars, "Don't think I don't support you because I don't come to the chapel." I laughed. "Chief, I'm glad that you don't come to the chapel." Chief was my friend. If the day arose that he needed a chaplain, I would have to do the same thing for him that any friend would do. I'd have to find him a chaplain. I couldn't be that person for him.

Failure 2: The Game of War

In June, I got careless, even reckless.

Camp Taji was quiet. In May, there had been only a smattering of suicide bombers outside of our gates. Those events had come nowhere close to us. The attacks were limited to the main front gate. The US portion of the post was miles away from that gate, but that didn't prevent ISIS from attempting to breach it. Though no US military were harmed in these assaults, each event took the lives of several Iraqi soldiers and other local contractors. It was a strange phenomenon to have no connection to the forces losing their lives for our security. The explosions rarely even triggered our base defense protocol.

After a while, it was easy to dismiss the enemy completely. Suicide bombers were devastating, but their blast radius could not reach us. We were deceptively safe. It seemed like ISIS did not possess any weapon system that would be able to reach us. Since so much of the fight was west and north of us, it didn't even feel as if attacking Taji was a tactical objective of the Islamic State anymore. I turned my mind off during the daily briefing on threat levels and enemy activity.

Once I went to bed and woke up enough times with this perception in my mind, I began to tell myself that I was actually safe. I even speculated in my journal whether I was safer here in Taji than I was in Tucson. It was arrogant, but time and complacency were natural bedfellows to such hubris.

Evidently, I wasn't the only one growing increasingly comfortable. On Taji, we had this strip of stores cobbled together with wood decking. We called it the boardwalk, since it hinted at the ambiance of Southern California beaches sans the ocean, plastic surgeons, and lifeguard shacks. The stores did sell overpriced coffees and fruity-flavored fake beers, so that was a nice touch.

Every night, the boardwalk was packed with military personnel from all the coalition forces eating, drinking, and smoking from hookahs. There they sat under multicolored lights as Iraqi music played softly in the background. With the soldiers' guns politely stowed under tables and chairs, one could be forgiven for thinking we were far, far away from a combat zone.

I found diversion on these nights playing sports with other soldiers. There were impromptu tournaments for softball, volleyball, and basketball. One of the contractors was even able to find plastic medals and T-shirts for the winners. I brought home a collection of them for the kids to play with.

As I walked to another game or store along the boardwalk, I would pass deteriorating bunkers and/or a lazily manned gunner's nest. From the look of the defensive positions, it seemed like it had been years since this portion of Taji had been attacked, which was a relief but also unhelpful. I marveled at the irony that our relative safety probably subverted our actual safety.

Before I knew it, I started treating the deployment as if it was an elaborate training exercise. It was like a game. If you were good at it, then the Army even gave you a medal for it at the end.

But then life in a combat zone gives you a little reminder: This is real.

For me, this happened in June when I woke up in a distant western FOB to the sounds of an artillery barrage. The tent shook with each charge. I could feel the hair on the back of my neck. I stood, quiet.

"Outgoing," the sergeant stated as he continued to fold his laundry. The cannons were half a mile away, but they shook the whole camp.

He must've noticed that his words were not reassuring me. "Incoming rounds come with a siren. You are good, Chap," he smiled.

A few days passed and I returned to my preferred status of complacency. The barrage was always outbound. The war was always far away. The enemy was safely distant.

Later that week, I had the opportunity one morning to visit the soldiers manning the cannons responsible for the outgoing munitions. They were a good group and proud of their expertise and teamwork. Each cannon looked like a tank. It was enormous. The shells they fired were equally large and heavy. One of the NCOs walked me through the process.

"You get a notice to fire, along with the coordinates." He showed me the computer. The space in which we were crouched was barely large enough for two people.

"All the information you need is in the message, like what type of shell to use," he added. "Then you load the shell here, coordinate the trajectory, let the commander know you are good to go, and then wait for the final order to fire, which we do by pulling the cord."

As he was telling me these things, an order came through. The mood switched gears. Soldiers sprang into action. I began milling toward the back. Before I could leave, the crew was ready. They were fast. They were just waiting for the final order.

"You want to pull the cord, Chap?" he shouted over the cranking noise.

"Seriously? Sure," I responded.

As I took up the cord, I felt this shame wash over me.

As a chaplain, I was a noncombatant. I had no weapon. I did not participate in offensive maneuvers. I was not trained to kill. Back in the States, when the unit went to the range, I never fired. Not once. If offered the chance by another soldier, my response was always the same: "Every round I put down range is a round you aren't putting down range. You need the training. I don't. My safety depends on your expertise. Aim true."

But there I stood with the cord. This wasn't a range. If I pulled the cord, I would potentially be ending the life of someone at the other end of this shell's arc. I was mortified. This wasn't a game.

Like most men, I rarely learned from my mistakes the first time. After lunch on that same day, I ran into some of the SEALs preparing to meet with some of the local militias. We talked basketball, but then they offered to take me with them outside of the Green Zone.

"It's not a big deal. We aren't going outside the outside wire. Just outside of the US wire," the officer said coolly.

"That'd be great. Let me grab my chaplain assistant."

"Oh, we only have room for one," he answered. "We got you."

These guys were Navy SEALs. They had more training than my chaplain assistant would ever have in his career, I reasoned. So, I jumped in the vehicle.

We arrived at a barn-like structure. There were soldiers from the FLE moving shipping crates of uniforms and arms. There were Iraqi military personnel walking about smoking and talking.

I stood in the middle of this situation taking it all in. The thing was like a bad war movie. There were soldiers lumbering around in mismatched uniforms with stars and eagles and stripes all over their uniforms. There were men standing with AK-47s, speaking in muffled Arabic as they viewed the items being delivered to the militias. It was fascinating.

At some point, I looked around and the team with which I'd ridden had gone to an office in the back and had accidentally left me. As I looked around the room, it occurred to me that I was the only US military personnel presently in the room. It also occurred to me that I was the only one in the room without a weapon. At that moment, I don't think I took another breath. Also at that moment, I heard my BC's voice in my head reminding me why he hadn't taken me outside the Green Zone on key leader engagements with the local Iraqi military back in Taji: "You are a high-value target because of the cross you wear and the propaganda videos that could be made with them catching a 'crusader' among us."

I'd messed up. I'd let down my BC. I'd let myself down. Ultimately, I let down my family at home praying every day that I would return home unharmed. And yet, there I stood, treating war as if it was some sort of game.

On this day, I would be fine. The SEAL guys were maybe gone a minute. The Iraqi figures were all allies and had no intention of doing me harm, but it was an inexcusable place to be. The BC would be displeased at me later that day when he heard I had gone out, and rightly so. I wrestled with this the rest of the night and for the next several days.

When I got back to Taji, I went and climbed the stairs to the roof of an administrative building. I looked out at the horizon as the sun was setting on the post. Although I could see for miles, I still couldn't see beyond Taji. I started to smell the aromas rising from the hookah bar. The glow from the boardwalk was growing stronger, but I looked at it differently now.

One last time I looked out. I thought that if I looked hard enough, I would be able to see my family. Instead, all I could see were the many lives that had been lost on this military post over the years. Many of those faces were US soldiers. People had died where I now stood. My cavalier attitude had to go. It was disrespectful not only to those who had actually died but also to the families whose prayers for a safe return went unanswered. I walked away from that moment a better chaplain, soldier, and human.

I walked downstairs like the sun walking down on the horizon. I thought of the cock's crow ending not only another day but also Peter's failed mission. I imagined that he probably thought every mistake would end with a conversation with Jesus that went, "So, Peter ... Look, I don't think this is going to work out." In hindsight, I bet he forgot all the stupid little things he'd told himself he'd never forget. In the end, I suspect that the only failure that stuck with him were those denials. But I wonder if he ever knew that the lessons he learned from that moment would shape a legacy of calling in which one day people like me would share. I wondered, too, what effect my failures would have among the lives and places I'd served.

Failure is a complicated gift.

Chapter 11

The End Is Near: RIP/TOA

The daily brief had ended. People were starting to shuffle out the doors. There were the usual sounds of chairs scuffing on wooden platforms and soldiers laughing at jokes they had been holding in during the meeting. The room smelled of coffee, dirty laundry, and gunmetal. There was a reassuring rhythm to the battle update briefs. I wondered whether I was going to miss them, the familiar faces and the running jokes. We were hours away from welcoming our replacements into Iraq. Already, the new unit was in Kuwait being in-processed. They were a reserve unit too, and like us they were a hodgepodge of specialty MOSs from around the country. I imagined that they were just as disoriented as we were when we arrived.

At least they would be able to have confidence in their mission. We had been able to have a few secret-level conference calls and video meetings with them while they were still in the States. The replacement unit had even been able to train on some specifics while they were still at North Fort Hood. They were fortunate. They would arrive prepared for more knowns than unknowns, and they would also be inheriting some key staff positions.

At that morning's daily briefing, I offered these words from Henri Nouwen:

> Hospitality means primarily the creation of free space where the stranger can enter and become a friend instead of an adversary. Hospitality is not to change people but to offer them space where change can take place. It is not to bring men and women over to our side, but to offer freedom not disturbed by dividing lines.

As our minds fought the temptation to check out, our mission was ramping up for a new push into enemy territory. There would be a new FLE inserted into Syria as ISIS was forced out of Mosul. The amount of cognitive focus, logistical planning, and sheer energy to open up a new front was intense. I marveled at our team's capacity to wade through the malaise of those final days in order to establish this functioning supply hub.

We were all close to being out the door when the battle desk captain yelled out, "We need all RIP/TOA slides by COB (close of business) today!"

RIP/TOA. How sweet-sounding a name that promised to save me!

As I understood it, RIP/TOA stood for Relief in Place/Transfer of Authority. This Excel spreadsheet outlined each section's process for handing off their section to the incoming replacement. There were cells for each item that indicated whether the task was done and where you and your replacement were on a particular line item. This gave the battalion leadership an ongoing snapshot of how the transition was going and directed their attention to items that might need additional support or guidance. RIP/TOA was a magical term. It meant we were going home. I had fun creating other definitions of the acronym, like Righteous Infighting Prevents Toddling Officers' Aggravations, but none could capture the power of knowing that it's all almost over.

Over the last month, other units and their task forces had begun to switch out. I watched friends falter under the strain of these transitions. Evidently, it was challenging to give up a mission which had been critical to your existence for a significant period of time. These soldiers had put their hearts and their values into their work. With RIP/TOA slide decks in hand, the departing soldiers were answering myriad questions about the whys and the hows. All of the unit's work was being dissected and evaluated by a fresh set of eyes seeking to make their mark on the war effort.

I was naïve. I figured that the warm handoff came with warm feelings. I had theorized that one's replacement would be grateful for all the work and for the tested and proven processes a unit had relied on for success. I was seeing a different story play out firsthand with the various units initiating their RIP/TOAs. In some cases, it was brutal.

"Oh yeah, Chaplain!" Major XO took a break from his buffalo chicken sandwich. It was Sunday, and the DFAC always served these on Sundays. I was going to miss the DFAC even though security in ours had been elevated after the chow hall bombings in Afghanistan a few weeks earlier.

"I can promise you that the new unit is going to come in and assume that all our shit is jacked up," he added.

Chief chimed in, "It's the Army way. You think you know better than the guys you are replacing."

I finished my sandwich. I would miss them. I would also miss Saturday-Night Stir-Fry and Taco Tuesdays. I despaired at the thought of not having my daily breakfast and cherry pancakes.

"Well, damn." That was all the insight and wisdom I could contribute. My grandfather used to say that *well* was a deep word for a shallow man. I definitely felt like I was up to my neck in something.

Later that night, after the evening chapel service, I was a blustery mix of nervous excitement and troubled speculation. These feelings and emotions were exhausting. I was making myself tired, and I was sure that I was making others fatigued as well. On deployment, there was a persistent pressure to stay motivated. I was stumbling with this pressure.

So, I went for a run on the treadmill, and I thought about transitions in leadership. I wondered about Moses and Joshua. During different phases of my life and ministry, I have had different attitudes about how Moses climbed a mountain to his eventual demise, even after all the years and the risks associated with leading the Israelites to the banks of the promised land, and how he watched Joshua take the people across the way to live into a promise of God's making.

In seminary, I remembered writing a paper about the injustice of it all. How can we preach about an equitable and loving God if, after all that, Moses was banished to die alone? Where was the fairness within this scripture? Where was the reward? I wrote about how petty God seemed in these passages. Did God just use this man and then throw him away? Was that what I could expect of God as I formed my call in service to God's kingdom? I was unnerved.

Then my perspective on this moment in Moses' journey changed again after a very painful departure from a church. I projected my experience once again onto the text. I watched Moses climb that mountain with relief in his steps that he would no longer be responsible for a recalcitrant people. I had spent years trying to transform a church from a Christian social club to something more dynamic, bureaucratically lighter, and more faithful to the needs of the downtrodden around us. As I took my wounded pride and battered calling out the doors that final time, I was relieved that I no longer had to circle in the wilderness with them. I relished the thought of climbing a mountain and watching them carry on without me.

As I, running, retrieved that scripture into my heart, a new question came to mind. I wonder how Moses felt about having to hand off to Joshua. Was he apprehensive? Did he believe that Joshua could handle all that he'd done? Was Joshua worthy of the journey he was about to make? What did Moses' RIP/TOA look like? Was Joshua standing there thinking that he could have gotten the people to this point in half the time? Did he plan on using anything from his time with Moses, or was he ready to put his own mark on the movement into the promised land? I couldn't find peace in any of the answers I imagined.

Later that night, I found these words by T. S. Eliot: "For last year's words belong to last year's language / And next year's words await another voice ... And to make an end is to make a beginning."

A week later, on Saturday, December 17, I received a text: "They are here!" It was surreal. My heart was pounding. My mind raced. I grabbed my hat and took off to the billeting office, where the unit was being assigned their CHUs.

I arrived to find a bewildered group gingerly placing their bags upon the ground. Many of them were checking and then rechecking their weapons, making sure that their defensive posture reflected the new threat level of being in Iraq. Most of them still had their vest and helmets on tightly. They spoke quietly within huddled masses, waiting for the next command from their leaders. I watched as their eyes scanned the post, knowing that everything probably just looked brown, dirty, and nondescript. I laughed to myself even as I sought to hide my grin, since I didn't want them to think that I was mocking them. I wondered whether I had looked as scared and uncertain as these soldiers did now. I am sure that if I could've tracked down the contractor who'd welcomed me to Taji he would have answered in the affirmative. Here was another Reserve group pieced together. They were younger than our unit, and I scanned the crowd and wondered which would be the ones that succumbed to the pressure, the soldier issues, the early dismissal, the career killers. I said a quick prayer for them.

After a search, I finally found their chaplain, my replacement, my ticket back home. He was tall and confident looking. He appeared ready. I exhaled for what seemed like the first time in thirty minutes. As I shook his hand, I felt an energy and a joy that had been absent from me for a month. It was humbling. I guess I hadn't realized till that moment how emotionally, spiritually, and physically exhausted I really was. As we exchanged pleasantries, I felt renewed. I prayed for him with every fiber of my being at that moment. I prayed that he would be successful. I prayed that he would be safe. I prayed that God would guide him to the places of the soldiers' greatest needs. I prayed that he would be a presence of grace in a place where grace is often hard to come by.

We located his chaplain assistant. She was tall and assured in her presence too. Her movements and speech were quick, and I could tell from their demeanors that they had forged an excellent working relationship. I grinned as I hypothesized about how long it would take before they realized that they didn't need to walk around in tandem everywhere. Part of me—a very small part of me—was jealous of the journey that they were about to undertake. Let the great RIP/TOA begin!

As I stood there talking with them, my mind raced with all the things I wanted to say. I could see the words and the spreadsheets and the chapel schedules all spill out from my brain onto the muddy mix of gravel and dirt there in the parking lot of the billeting office. I kept talking and talking and talking. At some point, I had enough self-awareness to see the glaze fall over their eyes, and so I shut up. In Army parlance, the next week was going to be like "drinking water out of a fire hose." I enthusiastically shook their hands one more time. I needed to make sure one more time that these two who stood before me really were flesh and blood. Satisfied, I sauntered off through the arriving nightfall. It was Saturday night. Cigars with Chief awaited.

The next week was an absolute blur as we all hunkered down with our replacements. I did not see much of my friends during the day since working lunches and dinners had become the norm as every staff section tried to distill every helpful thought, product, or process for the new unit. Most nights, Chief, XO, and I would still stand outside by our fire ring and smoke cigars. We would catch up on the day's occurrences. There was laughter and there was a recognition that nights like these were numbered too. It was emotionally complicated, and I didn't understand how to process all the feelings that I was having.

I would still go through many of the same routines as I had during most of the deployment, but I noticed a reluctance on my part to form new relationships. I would meet someone playing basketball and I would not really care to learn his name. New division leaders would come through and want a tour of the Resiliency Center, and I would pass off the task. In fact, I rarely visited the Resiliency Center anymore as new people, new programs, and new services began to close an old chapter in order to start a new one.

My replacements were fortunate. Many of the RIP/TOA tasks would not be applicable to them. Moving forward, they would only have to function as a battalion chaplain team. Some general somewhere was pushing north a dedicated chaplain team with a field-grade ranked chaplain at the helm. They would be charged with creating the programs and services. They would be the team to provide coverage for the units located on Taji without a chaplain. Sadly, this team would arrive after I left, so there would be no RIP/TOA with them. My replacement would only be tasked with the occasional chapel service, but the rest of his time and bandwidth would be for his battalion.

It took me several hard days to make peace with the inevitable fact that the replacement chaplain would do things differently than I had. This became crystal clear at one of the battle update briefs when his chaplain assistant offered the thought for the day. I had spent months exposing soldiers to Dostoyevsky and Hemingway and Toni Morrison and other philosophers. As I sat there that morning and listened to her read a lyric from Bone Thugs-N-Harmony, I swallowed a need for control that I knew would no longer help me.

Each day, we pulled out the RIP/TOA and made progress. I took the new chaplain around to introduce him to the individuals, both military and contractors, who could help him along the way. I showed him some shortcuts around the post and mostly enjoyed sharing in his enthusiasm for the mission ahead for him. With each meet and greet or lesson on troop movement, I experienced this bittersweet emotion. I loved the soldiers and contractors I served. I would miss this place.

And then one morning it happened. I walked up to the same door that I had been walking up to for months. I punched in the code. I walked to the next door, punched another code, and made my way down the hall. I greeted a few familiar faces, but as I peered into the various offices, most of the desk were now staffed by the replacements. The keys were struck on dusty keyboards with confidence and direction. The phones now bore the call signs of the new unit. When they answered, they no longer had to explain who they were. This was their building. This was their mission now.

As I turned the corner to my office, I heard soldiers laughing from the chaplain office. I entered, grabbing a cup for coffee. The voices quieted, and one by one they exited. I brewed a strong cup of premium coffee. As I turned, I was met by the gaze of my replacement and his assistant.

"Good morning," I said pleasantly.

In my mind, I ran through the few remaining items I figured we'd discuss today before I took a long lunch and maybe played some basketball.

"Good morning," the chaplain assistant responded.

"And how are you this morning, Chaplain Chandler?" the chaplain asked.

"I'm solid. One day closer." I took a seat in front of his desk.

I looked around the office. All the decor, the cards, the drawings that my children had drawn were down now. There were different things on the walls. There were lists and priorities of the chaplain team. There were a few whimsical knickknacks on the bookshelves behind the desks.

"What are you up to today?" the chaplain asked.

He rested his elbows on his desk as he smiled. He was well loved by his soldiers, and his easy demeanor was probably a significant factor in his appeal.

I opened my notebook. "Well, I figured we'd go over these last few items that we kind of started but probably need to finish up so that we can be done with the RIP."

I glanced over the one I thought would be the easiest to tackle. I made a mark through "visit the PAX terminal to introduce him to Clarence so that they can schedule their first flight." We'd done that two days ago. I read aloud a few options from the RIP/TOA slide deck.

"I don't know. What do you want to tackle first? You're in the driver's seat now," I said enthusiastically.

"You know, man. I think we are good," the chaplain answered.

"Okay. What about ..." I scrolled through the list again.

"Nah, I mean, I think we are done." He looked at me kindly. "We are good."

I didn't know what to say.

"You set us up for success." He looked over to his chaplain assistant. She nodded.

I was not ready to leave. I was not yet ready to take off the yoke of this role. I was not ready for my part in the mission to be over.

But it was.

"Good luck, y'all," I said heavily.

I placed the last of my coffee, still hot in the cup, beside the chair. I stood up and carefully made my way out of his office. I didn't make eye contact with anyone on the way out. I couldn't. I thought about the chaplain team behind me. They were good. They really were. I was done now. I was grateful. I was one day closer to a new chapter.

I imagined that Moses probably felt similarly, but on a larger and deeper scale. He had spent over forty years in his position. I had spent only three hundred days on this deployment in my job. All the same, I suspected that the day on which Joshua looked at Moses and said, "We are good, man," was a difficult one for Moses. I doubt the weight of it was due to any disbelief in the ability of Joshua. Moses knew Joshua was set up for success. It was just hard to let go of a role that had shaped his identity so profoundly.

Thankfully, however, God gave Moses a new season of life. Though this would be a solitary one, and though it would be his last, it was no doubt a moment of gratitude. It was a time in which Moses could look with love and hope at all the sacrifices he had made that would be carried into the promised land. Those sacrifices would become the seeds of an ascendant future written by God. Moses' final moments on that mountain would be days filled with the freedom to remember that he wasn't the yoke that he carried or the cries of the people's journey. He was simply Moses, a child of God, his true self beyond the role that he was called to embody.

And so, Moses looked at Joshua and all the people gathered in that moment, the book of Numbers writes, and he said heavily, "Good luck, y'all."

Chapter 12

The Holidays at War:
Merry Christmas, Maybe

Christmas morning in Iraq sucked. There was no way to dress it up. I wished that I could, but that would have been disingenuous. The old-timers had forewarned me. They grumbled, "It's brutal on the guys who have little kids back home … fucking worse for the moms walking around here." Then their eyes would drift forlornly: "You don't get those years back, sir." Soldiers are surprisingly articulate with their internal dimensions.

On December 25, I opened my eyes to a cold, grey world. I could hear the rain hitting the metal roof. It had been raining for days. Taji wasn't a scenic destination under normal circumstances. When it poured as it frequently did during the rainy season, these war-torn grounds looked like a dystopian B movie. It was sad. I could already imagine the fog that awaited outside. Visibility, already shortened by excessive concrete T-walls, would be restricted even more. When I complained about the fog one morning, one of the interpreters having coffee in the chapel joyfully replied, "Fog is God's blessing that gives us a break from having to look at this godforsaken land!"

Our transient room was empty. We had been moved there to make room for our replacements. My roommate was spared most of the stay in this rusty and pungent cube. He leveraged his excellent work in Iraq to get an early ticket home to start a new assignment back in the States. This room looked very similar to the one I had lived in for the entire deployment except that there wasn't a protective concrete overhang. Fortunately, the mortar "incoming" sirens had remained silent for months, so we carried no anxiety into these new accommodations. We were all just too tired to care anymore. We were as exhausted as the rooms appeared.

All of my personal effects—the drawings from kids, the post-cards from friends, all the things you place around you in your CHU to create home in the middle of an FOB—were packed up. I had packed these items with almost sacred care. They had meant more to me than the senders likely ever imagined possible. As I stared at the ceiling, listening, a bare mattress underneath me covered in God knows what, I was overcome with a simple, sad realization: I was alone and I felt alone. During these moments, I wrote these optimistic words in my journal:

I don't want to be here. I cannot believe that I'm here. I cannot be-lieve that my children will awaken on Christmas without me. Forgive my despair, God. S---. Amen.

All the traditional signs of Christmas were missing. Back in the States, we lamented the gross commercialization of Christmas. We rolled our eyes when we walked into big box stores in September to find familiar holiday decor being hung. I shared the concern, but I understood why they did it. The promise of these symbols is powerful. One realized that when they were absent. I looked into my darkened room. There was no tree in the corner. In its place were cakes of the infamous Taji mud. There were no gifts. We were so close to going home that I had asked the family to save them at home. There were no kids anxiously sleeping in the next room. There were no late-night construction projects with my spouse gently taunting me. I felt the distance of this moment acutely.

When those old-timers shared their experiences, there was routinely a heaviness in their presence. I felt this weight now. I don't know how they did it. For some, this was their third or fourth Christmas away from home. It happened so frequently that Christmas had ceased to carry the whimsy, wonder, and expectation of most people's holidays. War had scarred it. For these soldiers, they no longer even speculated about what this was like for their families back home. They didn't arrange for any surprises. They numbed themselves to these days and tried to think about it as little as possible. In their hearts, they turned to the future. They would hopefully have another shot at creating Christmas magic later in life with their grandkids. I wondered whether that would even be possible; they seemed too acclimated to the fog of Iraq.

I looked at my watch wistfully: 0630 hours. Already the most miserable Christmas of my life.

Merry Christmas, ugh.

Chaplains didn't get to sulk. At least, not for long. One of the things with which I quickly had to come to terms as a chaplain (and to some extent this was true in civilian ministry as well) was that when an entire military unit was downtrodden due to the context around us, one person has to carry the torch of hope and perseverance. Somebody has to do it or morale will slip quickly. Fair or not, the chaplain is expected to be that one person. I pleaded with myself to remember a familiar theme: There was an opportunity for meaning in every moment. I drove this idea into every searching soldier I met. That's the narrative of Christmas, right?

So ... I got up. Sort of. And I read from my journal. I forced myself to remember. I knew that the last month had been filled with beautiful, unexpected moments of hope as we experienced Advent, the days leading to the promise of Christ's birth. I exercised remembrance because I needed the promise of Christmas in a way I had never before experienced. When I look back on it now, I realize that Christmas Day forced me to live the words of Christmas Eve and the road to it.

I have since concluded that Advent in Iraq may have been the first time I ever truly experienced Advent as it was meant to be experienced. Advent was a season of preparation and hope. Evidently, wading and waiting through a theological season of longing and hopelessness in a combat zone forces you to clarify what it is you expect to happen with the birth of Christ. That was the secret. Advent basically required an existential threat and soul-crushing separation from a longed-for future filled with love. Turns out that was exactly what most contemporaries of the original event were experiencing.

In my journal, I reflected back on the first Sunday of Advent, liturgically symbolized by hope. During my message on November 27, I had asked those gathered in chapel, "What are we waiting for?" I got a few knowing chuckles. Military life was a waiting life. We hurried and assembled and then we waited. We moved to a location and then we waited. It became ridiculous at times. I honestly believed that an E-5 (sergeant) wasn't allowed to pin on the coveted chevrons until they could master the deep and bellowing command, "Hurry up and wait." Back home, we were conditioned to think that life in a combat zone was like an action movie. The reality would be such a disappointment to the average moviegoer. The twenty-something books I read in Iraq suggested a much slower-paced movie! The irony of "hurry up and wait" was that it created dead space, which allowed boredom within the ranks. Boredom was an unwelcome friend. It tended to be the mistress of adrenaline-fueled bad decisions. A significant proportion of the counseling that I conducted was the result of soldiers managing their boredom ... unsuccessfully.

"So, what are you waiting for? Do you even know?" I asked again that morning. The fact was that most of the time that we were "hurrying up and waiting" in the military we didn't actually expect anything to happen. Indeed, most of the time nothing did happen. Soldiers carried the resentful perspective that leadership used the "hurry up and wait" command to buy them time to pull their heads out of their rear ends. Having seen the military from many different levels and perspectives, I think these soldiers were often correct. Now, as I preached these words, I had the sense that this line of questioning was an unfortunate metaphor for a faith community that had ceased to expect much of God's work in the world. We've settled. The birth of Christ rarely precipitates the birth of a new movement within our lives. Instead, it's a quaint celebration which gives us a reprieve from the stagnation we often live.

"Do you have hope that Christ's birth still matters?" I challenged them that day. These words were directed as much to me as those gathered there. Somewhere along the line of life, I had stopped living as if Christ's birth still mattered within my faith. I don't know when it had happened, but embarrassingly, I knew that it had happened. My suspicion is that it has happened to the majority of us. The faithful soldiers worshiping there that day bounced that question within their hearts and minds. As they did, I read these words from Paul's heart to the Roman church: "Salvation is nearer to us now than when we became believers ... let us live honorably as in the day."

Paul's words were humbling, at least on that day. It occurred to me that most of us go through this time of waiting without truly expecting anything, much less the birth of our salvation. We've turned Christmas into a relic. Christmas has become a celebration of a past reality rather than the declaration of a promised-for future. The point I was attempting to make that morning was that the waiting itself answers the question. The manner in which we patiently engage the weeks leading to Christmas revealed our belief about the question. Were we sitting around waiting to pull our heads out of our rear ends, or were we waiting because we were preparing to bring about a long-prayed-for future? I left the group gathered there in the chapel with a blessing and a hope: "Don't merely distract yourself and wait out these last weeks of our time together. Embrace the longing, the need for hope, the plea for peace, the brokenness of love and the desire for joy. Make ready for a real future where God is with us, Emmanuel."

I then went back to my CHU and cried. According to my journal, I woke up quietly sobbing every morning for the rest of that week. I wanted to go home, but I made myself live within the tension. I needed a new future, true, but I was going to participate in the blessing unfolding before me. I was challenged on this front after a particularly painful video chat with my younger daughter. She told me that she was only excited about Christmas because I would be home soon afterward. She passed the phone to my wife, and then I had to tell my wife that we'd been delayed a week. We'd be in Iraq a little bit longer. I wrote this prayer:

God, I will not lose hope.
Bring peace to the disquiet of souls longing for reunion;
Bring joy back to the lips of children created within your love.
God, I will hold on to you.
Forgive me for how I cling to you;
Forgive me for not being strong enough.
God, I will love through you.
Create moments of grace.
Create avenues for your mercy.
I need them.
Amen.

This was the beginning of Advent for me. Thanks be to God.

So, on Christmas morning, I glanced again at my watch: 0730 hours. I bounced off the bed. I grabbed a couple of pairs of pants. I put on the one that smelled the cleanest; I was done doing laundry at this point. In that muddy place, it was difficult to keep the clothes clean on the way back from the laundry point. I went for a walk. The rain had stopped, at least for the moment. I needed to create meaning in the name of the one we would gather to celebrate soon. Others would be feeling the same fog in their souls and mud in their minds. They could probably use a chaplain.

As I walked the FOB, I thought about all the ministry which followed that Sunday of hope. The days crept closer to Christmas Eve, and I lived the words I would preach in another sermon during this time: "Advent is an experience of the unfiltered wonder of God. In that experience, tragedy becomes the paradox of God's grace, the place where the eternal promise of God's peace is born." Every tear reflected the light of Christ's love. Every tragedy bore the mark of God's presence in the binding of difficult wounds. Every lament echoed within the grace of God's heart. It was both spellbinding and heartbreaking. I walked through the foul-smelling mud, bringing the reminder of a beautiful promise.

And it was needed. During those December days, my counseling load almost quadrupled. The reality of what many had ignored back home was catching up with them. Many soldiers soon learned that they had no jobs waiting for them back home. One might think those positions were legally protected. They were supposed to be, but there were ways around USERRA. For example, a soldier cannot be fired because of the deployment, but the soldier's civilian position can be eliminated as part of staff restructure. Marriages had ended in the last few weeks. One soldier's spouse had died. I cannot fathom the compounded grief of missing my spouse's last days due to the deployment. I cannot imagine the sadness of my last goodbye being a text message or distorted phone call. Perversely, not everyone wanted to go home. Some preferred to live in Iraq than face what awaited them back home, and so they secured roles with some of the units that were remaining in place. For them, it was easier to carry on in the strange certainty of Iraq. Throughout it all, I tried to stay rooted in God's grace as I held on to the grief of my soldiers.

The weeks of Advent stretched me the longer I lived within these moments of tension. By Christmas Eve I felt a sense of expectancy unlike anything I've ever experienced. I celebrated this all as I interacted with the soldiers I would soon be leaving. I was grateful for the witness we embodied. We all waited patiently for the birth of Christ, the birth of a tangible future in which we weren't entrenched in a war, fighting for the soul of the world. That patient waiting changed us. It shaped us. We felt more true, though I don't think that makes any sense even now. Thinking back, I don't know whether I could say that my prayers deepened or that my sermons were any more profound, but they were different. The best way to describe it is that they came from a different place within me than before. I can think of no better example than Christmas Eve, as I stood with incoming chaplains from around the coalition forces and a congregation from around the world. I wrote these words to a friend as I put the final touches on a Christmas Eve candlelight service:

The chapel is quiet right now. The only noise comes from the Black Hawks and Chinooks preparing to take off to destinations around Iraq. It is Christmas Eve. The rain is pouring, and the ground is rapidly covering in a type of mud that is anything but festive. It bogs down the mood of the camp, but the war effort does not slow. I have been here for every holiday this year. It never slows, not even in Taji, a place far from the thunder of the front lines.

In just a few short hours, the Australian padre, fellow US chaplains, and I will lead a candlelight service celebrating once again the birth of the Prince of Peace. We will sing traditional carols as military personnel and contractors from around the world pause to pay homage. It is a wonderful reminder. Men and women have looked to this event with hope-filled wonder for many years.

I think a great deal about peace these days. Whether it is Iraq or Syria, it is difficult for those who care not to watch with broken hearts. I feel fortunate to be part of an ongoing operation trying to do something about the tragedy we all see on our screens, but it never seems to be enough, and it never seems to move fast enough. The destruction is indiscriminate and especially brutal to those most vulnerable: the elderly, women, and children.

As I unpack the candles for the service, I meditate on the last year. I'm getting ready to leave. The battles still rage to my north and prob-

ably will for some time to come. There is a certain guilt I cannot help but feel as I prepare to leave. I get to go home. I get to hug my wife and children and sleep in relative safety under the beautiful Tucson night sky. If I want, I do not even have to consider the war-torn events I am poised to leave. It is a strange luxury lost on most of our country. I am ill at ease with that reality. And so, I wonder and pray: What will peace look like for this part of the world?

One of the officers at lunch recounted the story of the Christmas truce from WWI. I Googled it when I returned back to my office. The story perfectly illustrates how, during the weeks leading to Christmas, tragedy becomes the paradox of God's grace. The story has the feel of myth. As it goes, roughly a hundred thousand British and German soldiers were involved in an unofficial cessation of hostility along the Western Front. The Germans placed candles on their trenches and on Christmas trees. Both sides joined in singing Christmas carols, shouting greetings across the way. They even made excursions across no man's land to exchange gifts of food, tobacco, and alcohol.

How were they able to peer past their training and their reality to see the peace being celebrated in the birth of Christ? I think of the enemies we now face and I cannot imagine a similar scene. I cannot see the same opportunities for makeshift sacred space or a common understanding of humanity. During the Christmas truce, there was a stalemate in the trenches. There was a space created in the impasse. The space was steeped in desperation and prayer. It became a sacred moment juxtaposed with the coming Christmas morning. There was actually time to consider the story of the one hunkered in the opposite trench. The soldier was drilled to believe that the enemy soldier was the enemy of all life and all future. But in the space in between, they saw a common humanity. They saw the image of God within the other. In a season in which we celebrate hope, joy, and love, peace overcame them, even if for only a short while.

In some respects, it is probably not completely fair to compare this current conflict with that one so long ago. As I hear the approaching steps of a chaplain, one cannot help but wonder, however. Have the last thirteen years of war created a similar type of stalemate? This deployment has created more questions than answers. Will we be able to take the tragic spaces created by war and make them holy? How will peace be possible if we are unable or even unwilling to see our own stories, sons, and daughters in the faces of our enemy? I do not know. In our candlelit circle tonight, there will be no elements of the enemy. There will be no echoing songs coming from battle lines afar. No gifts. No sharing of photos of family. No laughter. After nine months, however, I can attest that the same desperation and prayer will be here tonight.

The problem of peace is nothing new. I had hoped that this problem would be one I would not have to pass down to my children awaiting my return. I imagine that same hope was a driving reason for the anticipation surrounding Christ's birth so long ago. And so, tonight we will sing. And we will pray. And we will lift the light of Christ high into the air. And we will welcome the Prince of Peace, trusting like those soldiers did a hundred years ago that peace can be born in the most hopeless places.

The songs, sights, and smells of Christmas Eve left an imprint on my soul, for "the people who walked in darkness have seen a great light" (Isaiah 9:2).

The thoughts of the night before guided my path on Christmas Day. I felt my heart comforted. I carried the blessing of Advent and the promise of Christmas out into Camp Taji on this holy and sacred day. I prayed for guidance and that somehow I might reflect a blessing beyond me. I stopped by all the units and delivered snacks. I told funny stories. I'm sure some of them were ones that I had told them before, but no one seemed to mind. I even cajoled some of the stodgiest of sergeants into singing silly holiday songs. We were privileged to enjoy the day free of enemy intent. My Christmas Day required no breach of no man's land, but all the same it was a wonderful blessing. How many chaplains, much less ministers, have been privileged to preach the mysterious wonder and promise of Christ's birth in the middle of a war on Christmas Day?

Later in the day, the fog eventually lifted, though the rain returned. We opened up the chapel and busted out the mop buckets for all the mud. I didn't expect many worshipers since units were trying to keep their soldiers busy. Even the dimmest of leadership knew that Christmas wasn't the best day to have soldiers "hurry up and wait," so they were creating things to prevent boredom.

For those who came, we gathered for a simple worship service on Christmas afternoon. It was sparsely attended, but we had a beautiful time together. Part of the security forces from the Fiji Islands came and sang a few traditional Fijian songs. I have since reread the sermon I wrote for that day, and though it wasn't any good, it remains one of my favorites.

I began with another question: "What does Christmas now mean for us who waited for the birth of our Lord in a far and dangerous land?" Most of those who were gathered were ones preparing for departure like me, and like me their thoughts were filled with reflection. "In fifty years, I'll tell stories from this last year, especially of these last services together and the long wait of Christmas morning. I'll tell them to my grandchildren, and I'll try not to resent them as they roll their eyes: Another story from Iraq!" We all chuckled. Those who had deployed before had told me about the challenge of carrying stories that no one would want to hear after about a month.

"What does Christmas mean for us? It means that eternal hope is born in tragedy. It means that there was a time when the world could have resigned itself to living in darkness, but instead it welcomed the birth of God's love incarnate. It means we don't have to create hope, because God delivers it, and so we stand boldly to help nurture it. It means we will have to continue to stand together and beg people to remember days like today as we stand shoulder to shoulder, lifting the light of Christ up and out into the world." I ended the short sermon with hope and a prayer: "Take the light of this moment back home with you."

I then closed up the chapel one last time and went out to walk the FOB again. It still did not look like Christmas. There were no lights adorning the CHUs or Christmas trees in the windows. It smelled like Taji mud, which is a far cry from gingerbread. Despite all the appearances of Taji, it felt like Christmas, especially in the smiles of all those I met. I gave, and I gave, and I gave.

At 1600 hours, an alarm I'd set on my phone went off. I looked again wistfully at my watch, but this time much more hopefully. I'd set the reminder for when the kids would be close to getting up in Arizona. It's true: You don't get those years back. Despite being heartsick at that realization, I was grateful for a variety of reasons.

For one, I got to witness the joy of Christmas morning over a video chat. The children's play was magic. I think everyone they had ever met sent them a present that year. God bless him: My father-in-law had built a swing set in the rain during the middle of the night for them. The real star was my wife, Emily. She created a day filled with warmth and love. She made sure all were included. Her love covered broadly and deeply.

I was fortunate. I was not without a memory of their faces and squeals, and they were not without a memory of seeing my face and hearing my voice. I was lucky. In years past, the military men and women didn't have that luxury. Early in the wars in Iraq and Afghanistan, Christmas was the letters, photos, and whatnot that came in the mail. In the mid-2000s, I had heard stories of soldiers standing in line for hours for the opportunity to make a ten-minute phone call. The technology just wasn't there. I still struggle to articulate why the separation from my family had sent me into such a tailspin earlier in the day, but it had.

I finished the call from the chapel. I closed the facility with a prayer, and I started to slush my way through the mud back to the CHU. I was all tapped out. The morning despair felt like a previous deployment. As I was nearing my room, I received a text message. It read that I was needed for a situation at HQ. I could only imagine what awaited me. Boredom had struck again, I speculated. It was probably a busted party filled with smuggled booze. Maybe it would be an illicit relationship between an officer and an enlisted soldier. The vagueness of the text and the length of the walk gave me ample opportunity to create some elaborate scenarios.

It was a ruse. My friends were there waiting for me. Chief and the XO shouted, "What did you think the emergency was?" I smiled. "The CSM got caught with that goat again?" We all laughed. CSM jokes are the best. For my money, they were second only to "your mom" jokes. We caught each other up on the events of the day. My friends surprised me with a gift: a stale cigar and a fake beer. It was the last of our stash. For hours that night we stood outside the building that had housed the deployment. It was the same place where we had stood for many nights over the last months. We told stories. We laughed. And then we told more stories and we laughed more. That moment was one of the great blessings of my life. I went back to my CHU. I cried. Christmas had arrived in force. A new future began that day. *There is an opportunity in everything,* I heard a familiar voice say. And then I slept for twelve glorious hours.

* * *

A final note: You may wonder what Christmas was like the year following a deployment. Did I carry the light home? Did I create meaning in every moment? Well, it was definitely interesting. I wondered whether I would seek to regain the focus and depth of Advent in Iraq or whether I would succumb to the busyness of the season within a church. I didn't do either. What actually occurred was a surprise. I wrestled with an unexpected internal spiritual tension between playful whimsy and theological simplicity. In the end, playful whimsy won. I just missed my children so much.

So, December, well, it was beautiful. Every minute of it was a gift that I savored. The tension was gone, as was the longing and weepiness. The waiting and theological pondering was replaced with some of the typical busyness of the season, but I didn't care. Mostly, I hugged my children every chance I got. I didn't fight my wife on the itinerary. She completely overscheduled our days with whimsy and magic, and it was exhausting, and it was wonderful.

I did my part too. I created an over-the-top Griswold-style Christmas minus Cousin Eddie. I put the biggest tree I could find in our living room and stared at it every moment I could. We caroled. We cooked. We watched old movies and new movies. We went out of our way to fill stockings with love and goodies. We even bought a puppy from a sleazy chihuahua-smuggling operation out of Mexico and managed to keep the fact hidden for two weeks. I gained fifteen pounds, and it was one of the happiest months of my life. I gave, and I gave, and I gave, except this time it was to my family.

To be sure, it lacked the theological depth of the prior year, but I don't know if that's an experience I get again. At least, that's what I am rationalizing. I imagine if another deployment takes me away from my family at Christmas, God will have another opportunity ready. I'm just thankful that I didn't squander my Christmas in

Iraq. I know now how overwhelming it feels to welcome Emmanuel in the fog of hopelessness and longing. I know now why the magi left everything to greet the birth of Christ. I know now why these moments hold a power able to bring together enemies. I know now that the birth of Christ creates a light that the darkness will never be able to extinguish. One day I will share with my grandchildren how hope is born of tragedy, and I will encourage them to stand shoulder to shoulder as they carry the light of Christ.

Chapter 13

The Love of Saguaro Christian Church: My Beloved Saguaro

The apostle Paul opened his letter to the Philippian church by writing, "I thank my God every time I remember you." He used some variation of this greeting in many of his letters to the various communities he established and served. As you read through the Philippians letter, however, you get a real since that his love for this particular church was unique. It was deep. It was abiding. It was as easy as the grace that centered their relationship. I often remarked during sermons that one could clearly sense that the Philippian church was Paul's favorite or at least the most endearing.

As ministers, we know that we aren't to have favorites among the churches we serve. We are called agents of Christ to journey with God's people in a very specific season of their communal walk. And yet sometimes the relationship that emerges is special. This was how I understood my relationship with Saguaro Christian Church. They were my Philippian church. They were a blessing. Iraq wouldn't change that fact, but it would test it and ask questions of it.

I didn't know whether our relationship would survive the deployment. Distance can challenge relationships even in the best of circumstances. I considered all of these things as I prepared for the tour, even from the beginning. That pre-deployment Thanksgiving had been an emotional blur. I would like to think that I was more present, more engaged, and more intentional, yet in my journal I painfully articulated that I was struggling. I was making a show of being stronger than I was in reality. I was trying not to reveal the depth of this turmoil. As I shared in that celebration of gratitude with my family, my mind was spinning—and it would stay that way for the next year. I existed in a mind that rarely slowed, and Iraq did nothing to change that personality quirk.

After I learned of the deployment, I felt the weight of the news. How do you let your world know that everything has been turned upside down? Just as I searched for the perfect words in order to tell my children and family, so too I anguished with how to tell the church. I was at a loss about Saguaro. Here is a small journal sampling of the questions I spent days in prayer and discussion about:

Do they want me to stay?
Do I want to stay?
Would it be in their best interest to terminate me?
Would it be in their best interest for me to resign and save them the turmoil of voting me out? Would it be in their best interest for them to keep me?
Would it be in my best interest to stay?
Should I try to influence their decision-making one way or another?
Should I see this as a sign to switch roles and move to the active component?
Should I see this as a sign and resign my commission within the Army upon return?
If I stay, is it because God wants us to remain in a relationship, or are we more afraid of not being together than whether we should be together?
What can I expect of them with regard to ministering to my family?
What role can the church expect of my family in my absence?
What pastoral care would the church expect of me while deployed?
What care could I expect from them during the deployment?

I lacked the clairvoyance to answer these questions, and this created a feeling of spiritual failure within me. I was a minister, but I could not hear God's direction beyond the assurance of a steadfast presence sticking with me through all the discernment. I kept putting out metaphorical fleeces reminiscent of the biblical story, but the experiment of faith was inconclusive. I exhausted myself. I am sure I overwhelmed my wife.

I tried reaching out to friends and colleagues.

"Why are you worried about all of this? It will be crappy for Saguaro, but they will get through it."

"It's not that easy."

"Your jobs are protected while you are gone. Like, legally shielded, right?" a colleague texted back after I told him that I was set to deploy.

I texted back, "Sort of, not really, but technically yes, but not me."

"So … Saguaro can ask you to leave? I am confused." I didn't blame him.

"Yes. They can ask me to leave."

"WTF!"

I would not say I was scared that I would lose my position with Saguaro Christian Church, but I was anxiously uncertain. Let me explain.

There is a common perception among the general public that Army Reserve and National Guard soldiers' civilian jobs are protected and guaranteed while they are off serving the country. USERRA, the Uniformed Services Employment and Reemployment Rights Act of 1994, is the legal reference which undergirds this perception. I am not a lawyer, but essentially what USERRA codifies is that a civilian employer must keep a soldier's occupational position or an equivalent position available upon their return from deployment. This act, I believe, represents the better intentions of the American public. Public sector positions, like law enforcement or teachers, are champions of USERRA, which is wonderful given the number of soldiers within those fields. Congregational ministers are not protected by this law. Many of the reasons I was given relate to our tax status as self-employed professionals and the line that separates the church and state.

There are other loopholes to USERRA. Lots of them. For example, you cannot terminate a soldier for deploying. If you are a skilled technician (X) for a company, then the company cannot terminate your position and rehire a skilled technician (X). If the company fills your position while gone, then the company has to let you back into the position.

For the companies, the work-around that I personally witnessed on multiple occasions in multiple fields was simple: Eliminate the position of skilled technician (X). Recreate a similar type of position to skilled technician (X.a.1) and hire the slot. The soldier would be notified that due to budget cuts or reorganization, their position was no longer available, and that the soldier would need to look elsewhere for work. The emails always ended with, "Thank you for your service." Sadly, as the deployment eventually neared the end, and as soldiers began preparation for reintegration, many soldiers sat in my office as they processed the betrayal and the panic of what to do next.

I remember one soldier sitting in my office on Taji as we processed that he had no job waiting for him when he returned home.

"This cannot be legally correct." I steamed.

"I don't know, Chap, but this is what they are saying," the soldier replied. Defeated. Angry.

"We need to get you an attorney!"

"Sir, I can't afford a lawyer. I change oil at an oil change shop," the soldier replied.

I stared in disbelief.

"I'll just have to find another job when I get back. But it's getting harder to find people to hire me."

That last comment I heard repeatedly. The easiest way to avoid USERRA was not to hire reservists or guardsmen in the first place. I knew that firsthand.

Prior to serving at Saguaro, as I navigated the search and call process (our denominational human resources placement protocol), the topic of my military duty had come up with each church. They were always curious about the month-to-month reality but specifically about the possibility of a deployment.

"Well, there are two wars going on, so it's always possible," I typically responded.

"Well, it was nice speaking with you," the search committee typically shot back to me.

I was not privy to these churches' deliberations, but it was noticeable that my conversations with them ended after these discussions. In each case, the churches in question called ministers with fewer qualifications than me.

My colleague was flummoxed as he helped me search for a way to discuss this with Saguaro.

"But I've seen so many signs promoting the employment of veterans."

He was confused.

"True, but actively serving reservist and guardsman aren't veterans in the same sense. They may be veterans of a war, but those signs are for veterans of wars who are no longer serving. Many employers want to wave the flag, but they don't want to have to work around the flag."

"The same is true for churches," I added before he could respond. "In fact, most of the Reserve and Guard chaplains I meet don't work in churches. I rarely meet a chaplain who also pastors a church, and even more rarely do I meet a chaplain who is either the solo pastor or senior pastor of the church."

I learned early in my military career that many congregational ministers lost their churches due to deployment. I was advised to come to terms and peace with this reality before raising my right hand years ago. Like many things in life, one just can't understand the weight of it until one faces the moment.

To be clear: Saguaro Christian Church could have terminated my position. But they did not.

Instead, this community of faith leaned into the opportunity before them. They became the ideal of what so many churches can do for our military men and women during this era of unending war. There were no blueprints for this. We just trusted each other, and we grew into the experience together. Here's how they did it logistically and compassionately.

The Logistics

Leave of Absence:

In concert with the gifted leadership of our denomination's middle judicatory office in Arizona, I was afforded a leave of absence for thirteen months. This included extra time on the front and back of the deployment so that I could focus on my family. Additionally, Saguaro kept me on the payroll until the Army payroll began, which alleviated a significant amount of financial insecurity, especially since it took a couple of months for my military pay to become consistent.

Then, two phenomenal ministers, good friends of the church and of mine, paused their retirements in order to split the task of providing ministerial support to Saguaro during these thirteen months. These two gentlemen saw it as a gift to their friend, their church, and their country. The interims were aided by an associate minister in the last months of her two-year internship with Saguaro. She could easily have checked out, but she gave Saguaro her fullest efforts until the end. The interims were also able to lean on another of our denomination's finest ministers who just happened to be teaching in the local school system. True to form, she brought a powerful sermon regularly to Saguaro.

Lay LEADERSHIP:

As the old saying goes, the church was the people, and the people were the church. Saguaro had and continues to have amazing people. The lay leadership during this time was exceptional. This deployment caught them by surprise, as it did us all, but they expressed no anger or frustration. They met this moment with a cool resolve, and it showed in their sustained efficiency and care leading the church. Before I left, the moderators pulled me aside and told me that they were going to do their best to lead so that I could be fully present in Iraq. They met the expectation that they set for themselves. It was powerful.

The lay leadership of Saguaro did more than tread water during my deployment. They did not make Iraq, or my family, or me their only ministry. Clearly, the reality of the deployment used a considerable amount of the church's bandwidth, but they never lost sight of Saguaro's mission: to be the active embodiment of our values; to continue to be intentionally sacred, missional, intergenerational, and inclusive; and to create a place of ministry where Saguaro's purpose intersects with the community's greatest need. Saguaro continued to grow. Saguaro continued to be church at a time and place in which there aren't enough churches living into the fullness of who they were called to be.

Staff:

Saguaro was never "just a job" for the staff of the church. Many of them were either members of the church prior to their employment or became members out of their love for the church. They were particularly loyal to the church during my absence. Regularly, they went above and beyond in order to help ensure that the little details of church life never fell through the cracks. They helped create consistency at a time of leadership change. They put in extra effort that few beyond their families even knew about.

The Christian Church (Disciples of Christ):

There were no blueprints or policy manuals for Saguaro during this time. Mercifully, we had the denomination. We had exceptional ministers willing to share their gifts. We had an engaged regional office. We had lay leaders that trusted themselves to lead the church. The embodied the theological idea that they were in fact a priesthood of all believers and thus equipped to carry on in faithfulness. In addition to these realities, Saguaro and I were able to count on the chaplain office of the denomination for wisdom and guidance throughout the deployment. Lastly, the pension fund of the denomination intervened and ensured that my future pension would not be adversely affected by my leave of absence from the church.

Saguaro is not the denomination's biggest church, nor am I a power player within the denomination, but many within our denominational structure provided help when we needed it. Saguaro will never forget that. Nor will I.

Saguaro's Love

Letters and Packages:

The saints of Saguaro became quite biblical and sent me letters—real letters, handwritten on paper and everything. Prior to the leave of absence, I told everyone that if anyone wrote to me, I would respond. I have a long record of sending handwritten notes to parishioners. This stems from my adolescence in Kentucky, where thank you notes were an absolute must. It didn't matter if the note was for a stick of gum ever present in an aunt's purse or money for college—we were drilled to write, to write promptly, and to write legibly.

Even now, I have three boxes of letters and cards that were sent to me from Saguaro. The messages they contained sustained me. One of my favorite lines from a letter I received said, "The pen is the plow that tills the heart." I wrote alongside it within the margins, "And the life which emerges is the truth that no war can kill." I love letters. I turned to these letters often, especially the ones that the church wrote to me as I was preparing to leave. They were filled with prayers and promises.

I can assure you that each person who wrote me received a handwritten note on the special stationary I had crafted for the deployment. I cannot stress enough how lifting and sustaining it was always to have mail on mail call days. Our postal team had fun with it. They would text me on mail days to tell me whether I needed to show up with a vehicle in order to get all my letters, cards, and packages back to my CHU. I often took the cards and used them as decoration to soften the austere surroundings. Saguaro even sent me an Advent wreath for my sparse chapel on Camp Taji.

As if all the letters and items that they sent me weren't enough, they also regularly sent mail and packages to soldiers who seldom received such items. About once a month, I got an email asking for a new list of names of soldiers who could use some love. At Christmas, many of the soldiers without families found presents waiting for them under the tree. The soldiers would come into my office with a letter in hand and ask, "So who is [name]?" I would smile and share stories of the beautiful saints of Saguaro. It was such a gift.

The List:

Saguaro created and maintained a list for my family. On that sheet of paper were individuals and companies to see to home maintenance needs, weekly food drop-offs, childcare, and a cleaning schedule. This list was critical. All of my extended family lives and works in Kentucky. All of Emily's extended family lives and works in Texas. I left Emily with our children, who were five, three, and almost one.

When the water pipes in the front yard burst, Emily had someone to call. When the HVAC system quit, Emily had someone to call. Once a week, there arrived a "meal" of items all cooked based on a list of the children's favorite foods. I use quotation marks intentionally because there was usually enough food for three to four meals. When the children's schedules conflicted, which they did on an almost regular basis, there were people who watched one of the children. Even today, my children have a strong emotional connection to the saints who shared trips to the park or chocolate muffins at the café with them. Once a month, a cleaning service would show up and help restore order to the house so that Emily did not perpetually feel overwhelmed by tasks.

Saguaro breathed grace onto my family. They did it without judgment. They didn't belittle us if the house was a wreck one week or if Emily missed a week of church because she was tired or had family in town. They didn't express anger or frustration when my children were expressing anger or frustration because they lacked the capacity to articulate or express their emotional states during the deployment. They just loved my family. Their love for my family freed me from considerable worry. I attribute much of my success in Iraq to the lifting of that burden.

Then there are the stories and actions that I will probably never know about. The deployment was filled with the intangible mercy that comes from small, simple actions and lots of prayer. The questions scribbled in my journal that started this journey never fell away, but they lost importance. All that mattered was that we were in the walk together.

Paul wrote, "In all my prayers for all of you, I always pray with joy because of your partnership in the gospel from the first day until now, being confident of this, that he who began a good work in you will carry it on to completion until the day of Christ Jesus." I understand this joy. I understand this partnership. I am thankful for Saguaro from a place within me that only God could create. Like Paul, I know there will exist a day when the sails of my calling will drift me away from Saguaro's community and mission. On that day, I will give thanks for them. They were the embodiment of what is possible when faithfulness is matched with resolve and a hope born of Christ's love.

Beloved Saguaro, my Philippian church.

Chapter 14

The Last Days:
I'm Coming Home

"Are you getting to go home?" Her question startled me from looking out the window.

I was lost in my mind on this final, mechanically delayed leg of the journey home. It was disorienting being interjected into the "real world" again. The terminals of LAX are considerably different than the PAX terminals of Iraq. All the people, the sensory overload, the color: It was overwhelming.

On our last flight, a group of us was upgraded to first class. We grinned with sleepy eyes as we settled into the oversized seats. Over the intercom, the pilot directed everyone's attention to us, and he had the plane give us a round of applause. "Welcome back our soldiers from Kuwait!" I laughed as one of the self-conscious enlisted soldiers mouthed to the back of the plane, "He f-----g means Iraq."

The woman next to whom I sat on this plane to Tucson was so normal, which felt disorienting. She was pleasant, clean. She had a presence that reminded me of my mom. I started to cry.

"Yes, ma'am, blessedly. It's been a long time." I muffled out the words as I met her eyes.

I looked down at my uniform and smiled. I had washed the worn-out thing twice before I had put it on this morning and it still smelled like Taji. I wondered if that smell would perpetually permeate all my stuff from this deployment.

Typically, soldiers are asked not to fly in uniform. It's considered a faux pas. In chaplain school, I had befriended a former infantryman as an unlikely battle buddy. He drilled it into me that only dirtbags looking for a free pat on the back wear their uniforms in airports. I had been hesitant to put the uniform on this morning, but the battalion commander told me this was an occasion to wear it, proudly.

"Oh ... You were deployed?" she asked politely.

"Yes, ma'am. I am just returning from Iraq," I responded.

"Iraq? We are still in Iraq?" She was nonplussed.

Eleven days earlier, I'd sent an encrypted text from Iraq: "I am coming home." The insertion process into a combat theater as a reservist had been a series of anticlimactic moments. The inverse was equally so.

Due to the secretive nature of war, we were not permitted to give specifics about our return timelines to our families, especially through email or social media. OPSEC, or operational security, is an acronym that basically means keeping secret stuff secret. Troop movements are secret.

There was no real way of knowing a concrete timeline anyway. We moved from Iraq to Kuwait temporarily as we waited for a contracted plane and for our equipment to be loaded onto freight ships. Then we were sent back to North Fort Hood to out-process administratively and medically. Since we'd still be on orders and living in barracks, we were advised not to meet our families there, since we would not be permitted to leave post with them. I had already been warned that it would be excruciating to be in the States but unable to see our families. Our time in North Fort Hood depended on our medical issues and luck. It might take five days, or it might take a few weeks. Individual soldiers would be sent home as they completed the process.

If we'd been an active duty unit, then at this point we'd have given our families a date. All the families would gather in a hangar or on parade grounds. There would be pomp and circumstance. The soldiers would all be together and would go home to be with their loved ones. There would be an official end to the deployment.

Our last day in Iraq was January 2, 2017, and it lacked finality. As I'd stood over my packed bags, I couldn't help but drift back to that hangar in Texas what seemed like years ago. Even though this was far from the last gathering we were going to have, this was one of our last full formations. Many would stay either in Iraq or Kuwait. They had been recruited to other units and missions. Reserve soldiers were constantly needed as stopgaps for other missions around the world. These soldiers seemed content with their decision, but I couldn't fathom not running back home to the family.

"Form up." We were past declarative shouts anymore.

We were tired. We were ready. In our minds, we'd already left.

The instructions were barked out as usual. Hard times for this. Warnings for that. Ubiquitous mentions of battle buddies filled in all the spaces in between.

"Company!"

"Platoon!"

"Attention! Fall out!"

Before the normal noise of men and women moving on with their lives could ensue, I shouted out loud enough for Chief to hear, "Victory or Valhalla?!"

A few of us chuckled to ourselves. I couldn't remember the last time we had actually sounded off with that slogan. We were all ready to retire that mess to the annals of history, right alongside "Plagues and Pestilences!" As the C-130 began to taxi, I wrote in my journal, "and so it ends."

Our time in Kuwait was blessedly short. There was a definite swagger to our gait as we bummed around Camp Arifjan. At least now we had earned the confidence in our voices. Though I spent most of my time drinking coffee with Chief, I visited a couple of the higher HQ elements to whom I had spent the last months sending reports. It was definitely an inflating experience to walk halls and know that people knew you. Soldiers, even officers who dramatically outranked me, treated me with a certain deference. As I visited the chaplain team of the XVIII Airborne Corps, the chaplain assistant sergeant major shouted out, "There he is! The legend! Chaplain Chandler!" They coined me, meaning that they gave me a special challenge coin that was a token of deep appreciation and respect, and they even wrote a letter of recommendation for the possibility of a transition to the Regular Army.

It was a very affirming few days in Kuwait, but I was ready to leave the day I got to stand in front of a plane named Elaine, the middle name of my wife and daughter, which would bring us home. As we climbed on that plane, I took one last look north and said a quick prayer of thankfulness.

The plane ride was surprisingly mellow. Everyone basically kept to themselves. I wrote in my journal, unable to sleep. At one point, as most of the unit snoozed, I heard the pilot tell us to look out the window. I did and watched as we flew over the Great Pyramid at night. The Middle East truly was beautiful.

In keeping with the theme of this deployment, the return couldn't be simple. On the trip over, we had made only one stop in Atlanta before departing for Kuwait. I learned our redeployment would take four stops: Crete, Ireland, Newfoundland, New Hampshire, and then finally North Fort Hood.

The flight into Crete was fascinating. Low clouds made for a foggy landing on this compact island. The airport opened a special terminal for us, and we shopped at the local airport stores. We stayed only long enough to refuel and check a few mechanical things. I bought my children some tacky magnets just because.

Our next stop was Dublin. The soldiers were excited about the prospect of having a Guinness. For hours, there was an unsuccessful lobbying attempt by the soldiers to the battalion commander to have him temporarily lift the ban on alcohol, General Order No. 1. I could see the anguish on his face. He wanted one as much as anybody, but he refused. As we sat in that terminal, a few soldiers conspired to take me drinking on the final return flights. I witnessed their disappointment when I shared with them my journey of sobriety. I sensed that they didn't actually believe me. I, again, bought some more magnets just because.

Hours later we arrived at night in the middle of what appeared to be a blizzard in Gander, Newfoundland. The airport was closed, so a few airport personnel pulled a stair walkway to the plane. As we exited, we were blown and covered in snow as we made the hundred-yard walk to the empty terminal. Like most of the unit, I'd packed my military winter coats in my luggage. This time there were no open shops or food vendors. We sat in a tepidly warm terminal and waited for the next command.

Eventually we made our way to our first stop back in the States somewhere in New Hampshire. We followed the same routine as before as we walked into the terminal, wondering whether there would be at least one shop open this time for snacks. I was one of the last off the plane, and as I turned off the jet bridge, I could hear applause and shouts of welcome. Members of a local USO and VWF chapter were standing in the gate area to shake our hands, give us hugs, and most importantly to let us pet the small pack of therapy dogs that they had brought with them. I was weepy as I bent down and buried my head into the coat of a labradoodle. There were mountains of food and coffee. Several of the local leaders made small speeches that were touching, and the battalion commander responded in kind on behalf of our unit. I was asked to close the moment with a brief benediction. It was not difficult to find words of appreciation and blessing.

Our final stop was quick in coming as I slept due to a full belly and a full heart. We landed late at night at the same empty terminal that we had left all those months ago. The bleachers were still pulled up. The only difference was that there was not an honor guard this time. In their place stood a general, a colonel, and a lieutenant colonel, my former battalion commander prior to the cross-leveling, and a collection of command sergeants majors. This command team was here to welcome us back and shower us with praise. I could tell that some in the group, especially the cross-levels who would be returning to units outside of this chain of command, were ready to head to the barracks, but I thought it was a beautiful display of leadership. The general coined me and a few others with a coin the size of a saucer. And then we headed to the barracks.

I don't remember much from those days at Fort Hood. I mostly slept and talked with my family. I didn't journal much. I can't even recall whether Chief went home before or after me. During the fog of that time, my in-laws came and visited me since they lived only a few hours away in Texas. They took me to lunch and caught me up on some of the family news I had missed. Over the last year, they had frequently traveled out to Tucson to help Emily with the children. Emily's older brother had helped too. My parents had done the same. As I sat, ate, and listened, I was full of gratitude for the way our families had stepped up to shoulder the burden of the deployment. I knew for a fact that my situation was not the norm. Most of my fellow soldiers didn't have the same type of support within their families. A smattering of the soldiers were in no hurry to get back because their families had been broken by the deployment. Their eyes were filled with dread at the prospect of returning home from the challenges of Iraq only to face relationships broken with no easy fix. I lifted them in prayer.

The only other thing I really remember doing was looking for a dog. Seeing the therapy dogs in New Hampshire and remembering the bomb-detecting dog at the PAX terminal in Baghdad had locked in my mind an idea: I was going to incorporate a therapy dog into my position as chaplain. I had remembered reading about an experiment with that concept at Fort Bliss. We had a dog at home, but that thirteen-year-old basset hound was comfortable in her retirement. So, in the in-between moments of standing in line, I started a conversation that would eventually bring to our home a beautiful German Shepherd puppy, Gerta.

I made it through all the medical checks quickly. There was this strong desire to just obscure any answer other than "I'm good to go" so that I could go home quickly. That's one of the tough parts about being a reservist. You have to get everything medically documented, especially if you are going to need additional treatment, but you just want to go home and see your family. On the active side, since you come back to the post where you live, there is time to see family and address all the health issues.

Late on the ninth day after leaving Iraq, I was given the all clear to go home. A plane ticket was secured. I would leave the next morning. That afternoon I called home with the news, and my oldest daughter, Harper, told me on FaceTime, "I have two suitcases full of stuff to tell you in my brain!" She had grown so much.

At zero dark thirty the next morning, about fifteen soldiers and I boarded a bus for the airport. Many of this crew were fellow Tucsonans who had been cross-leveled with me. The battalion commander was there to send us off. He would not be going home until the last soldier had been cleared. It was a muted morning both in climate and in the group's mood. I don't know what I expected. At the end of one week of church camp, there were tears. There are always tears. After eleven months and ten days, I thought I might feel something akin, but I didn't. All my emotional energy was being protected. I think the same was true of most everyone, although a couple of soldiers used the departing moment to share every frustration they had harbored over the deployment. I was sad for them, but I left that sadness on the curb as the bus pulled away for the airport.

* * *

"Will your family be at the airport?" my new friend asked as she sought to move on from her last question.

"They will. My wife, two daughters, and son will be there. I believe my church will be there too," I replied, and showed her a photo of my family that we had taken before I left.

I watched as she looked at my children.

"They are so young ..." Her eyes filled with tears.

"My wife was a champ. In many ways, her day-to-day was harder than mine."

Out of the corner of my eyes, I caught the first glimpses of the Tucson mountains. My heart warmed. I'd missed them. Soon we landed, and the woman turned to me one more time.

"Thank you for your service." She held her hand out.

"You're welcome." It was the first time since joining the Army that I felt as if I had truly earned the gratitude.

* * *

The Tucson airport is a very simple one. There are two elongated terminals that lead to stairs and to the baggage claim area. The airplane came to a stop and we exited. As I walked down the long terminal, happy, grateful tears began pouring from eyes. I finally reached the escalators leading to the baggage claim and most importantly to my family. I could hear happy shouts and loud applause as a beautiful group of familiar faces came into view.

Eleanor, my middle child, ran as fast as her legs would move to the escalator steps, screaming, "Daddy!" Harper was only a few short steps behind her. By the time I looked up, Emily and Sam were wrapping their arms around me. I was home. Oh my God! I was finally home. I peeked at my blond-haired son. He smiled. "Hi, Daddy." Sam remembered me!

I gave God every ounce of gratitude I could produce. Most of the time in life, when you are in the middle of such a happy moment, time speeds up. You blink and it's over. As I stood holding my family for the first time in a long time, I felt as if it lasted for hours. It was like an apology from God: "I am sorry that war exists. Here is what eternity feels like, tastes like, smells like, and looks like."

For the next thirty minutes, I moved around in a sea of love. My church had come to share in this moment. They had signs and cards and balloons and all the hugs I could handle. They had shared in the shouldering of this deployment too. I was grateful to be with them again. As we were readying to leave, I looked up, and in the distant corner stood the woman with whom I had flown in to Tucson. She was sobbing as she placed her hands together in prayer. We received her benediction.

For the next several days, all I did was play with the kids and sneak off to make love to my wife. It was magical. It was ours. These hours were among the happiest of my entire life, second only to the birth of our children. As I did in the moments when our children took their first breaths, I knew that our lives would be forever different. All of our hearts were scarred, but healing.

Harper and Elle especially were reticent to let me out of their sights. That first week, every night was a campout in our bedroom. It seemed ridiculous to put five people in a queen-sized bed, but we made it work—meaning I made it work: I slept at the foot of the bed next to the cat. We woke up each day and shared all the things we had been carrying in the suitcases of our minds for the last year. Once I emptied mine, I put that suitcase away, hopefully forever. I added to the prayers of gratitude in those days a prayer for peace. I prayed no other family would carry the scars which God was now healing in us.

Chapter 15

The Family Interview:
The Ones You Leave Behind

As I was writing this book, I decided that I needed a chapter dedicated to the voices and perspectives of my family. They earned it, and honestly, America needs to hear them, especially if it is our country's intent to engage in a perpetual war on terrorism. In many ways, my family was asked to sacrifice more for their country than I was. Emily, Harper, Eleanor, and Samuel were the minority within the minority of the deployment experience. We send young men and women into combat theaters. In my unit, fewer than half of us had children. Iraq shaped our family too.

We were sitting at a burger joint. Harper, Eleanor, and Sam, now eight, six, and four respectively, were eating hot dogs and comparing the drink concoctions they had made at the soda fountain. Emily and I tried to get their attention.

Me: Let's talk about Iraq ...

Harper's smile turned pensive. Sam tried to throw a fry at me.

Me: Do you remember when I went to Iraq?

At the time of the deployment, Harper (five), Eleanor (three), Sam (barely one), were young.

Harper: I do. It was sad.

Eleanor: I do too.

Me: Sam, do you remember when I was in Iraq?

Sam burst out laughing.

Sam: You were on a raft?

Me: No. Iraq.

Sam: You fell off your raft?!

Emily: Do you remember when daddy was gone a long time?

Sam shook his head no. He threw another french fry at me.

Me: What do you remember most about the time right before I left?

Eleanor: It was sad. I cried a lot. Mommy cried a lot too. We didn't want you to go.

Harper: I didn't understand why you had to leave at first, but Mommy said you had to go help some soldiers. I just remember crying and Mommy doing special stuff to make us feel better.

Sam threw another fry. Eleanor had a frown that was trembling.

Eleanor: I didn't want you to die.

Harper: Yeah. We were scared because it was a war.

Me: What's a war?

Harper: It's where two countries fight and kill each other, and the one that wins gets to win the argument.

Me: Did you tell Mommy that you were scared that I was going to die?

Harper and Eleanor shook their heads no.

Me: Did it feel like I was gone forever?

Eleanor: Yeah.

Harper: It did at first, but then it went by fast. I just remember Mommy getting us up extra early so that she could take everyone to school. You missed my first day of school.

Me: I did. It made me cry. I missed a lot of things. Mommy sent me videos and photos of the things I missed, which made me happy, but it also made me cry.

Eleanor: You were sad also?

Me: I was sad a lot, sweetie. I missed you all so much. It broke my heart that I missed your birthdays and recitals.

Eleanor: Yeah, I wish you had been there ... But I know the soldiers needed you.

Sam had completely checked out of the conversation. Whereas I am thankful that he will have no memory of the deployment, it is so strange considering how formative it was for the rest of us.

Emily: Do you remember how far Iraq is?

Eleanor: No.

Harper: Is it outside of the United States?

Me: I thought you had a map or something?

Harper: We did! Iraq was so far away. We had a map of the world and we put the pictures you sent us on the map.

Eleanor: I remember the camels!

Harper: I dreamed that they chased you.

Eleanor and Sam laughed.

Me: Did you like all the things I sent you? The letters? The photos?

Harper: We did.

Me: Did you feel like you got to talk to me enough?

Though Emily and I kept in almost daily contact through texts, emails, and calls, we intentionally only had family calls once a week on Sundays. For birthdays and stuff, I would try to call an extra time, but the calls were a blessing and a weight since they often made the kids as sad as they made them happy.

Harper: I think so.

Eleanor: I loved video chatting with you!

Emily: Do you remember what was special about our calls?

Harper: Oh! I do! It was special because we got to do Communion with you each week. I loved that.

Emily took Sam to the restroom. His face was covered in condiments and he had to use the restroom.

Me: How was Mommy during the deployment? Was she happy? Did she get sad?

Harper: Mommy was sad a lot at first, but then she wasn't.

Eleanor: She was happy and fun and smiled and didn't cry that much.

Harper: She stayed really, really busy and we got to do lots of extra things.

Me: Did Mommy get lots of help from the Nonnas and Gigis in our family?

Harper: They all helped out a lot. Uncle Dustin came for a long time and it was fun.

Emily and Sam came back to the table. Sam immediately stuck his clean hands in ketchup.

Me: Did all your friends know your daddy was gone?

Harper: Yeah. They were extra nice.

Me: Did any of your other friends have dads deployed too?

Harper: No. I don't think so.

Eleanor: No.

They had gone through this experience by themselves, unlike families within the active component.

Me: Were our church friends extra nice also?

Eleanor: Yep. They made us stuff like mac and cheese. And cookies.

Harper: The food was so good.

We all smile as Eleanor pretends to eat like a puppy.

Harper: Daddy, will you ever have to go back there?

Eleanor: We don't want you to go again.

I paused. I don't know whether I will have to go again. I cannot imagine a scenario where I don't end up deployed again somewhere down the road, but I didn't want them to worry about me.

Me: I don't think so. Not for a really long time. But sometimes the Army needs me to help them.

Harper: I wish they didn't.

Eleanor: Yeah.

Me: Were you mad at me for going? It's okay if you were.

Eleanor stopped making eye contact. She wouldn't answer the question. Harper looked down, but I could tell she wanted to say something.

Harper: I was at first. I didn't know why you wanted to leave.

Harper paused for a while.

Harper: But then I understood that the soldiers needed you.

It broke my heart to think that Harper and probably Eleanor thought that I chose the soldiers' needs over their needs.

I switched to a happier topic.

Me: Do you remember when I came home?

Eleanor jumped up in her seat.

Eleanor: We had a party. We went to the airport and watched the screens for you to walk down the stairs.

Harper: The whole church was there!

Eleanor: And then we saw you and I was so excited, and I ran and there were balloons and there were shouts!

Harper: We said, "Welcome home!"

Everybody was laughing, even Sam, who was still licking ketchup from his cheeseburger.

Me: Do you know what proud means?

Harper: Yes.

Me: Were you proud that I went and did all of that?

Harper: Yes, but it was sad.

Eleanor: It was sad.

Me: I love y'all.

Emily: We love you too.

Early the next morning, Emily and I put on a movie for the children, and she and I talked more. I recorded the conversation since it was a longer one.

I picked up the voice recorder.

Me: I'm here with Emily Chandler. She is still in her PJs, and the time is approximately 0930 hours.

Emily rolled her eyes and laughs sarcastically.

Me: Do you remember all the ramp-up to the deployment? Thanksgiving and the first phone call?

Emily: It's a bit of a blur now.

Long pause. She was trying to retrieve the buried memory.

Emily: I remember we were trying to get the kitchen put back together for Thanksgiving and you got a call. It was the Army. I watched as you went and sat down at the table. I could tell then it was something serious.

Long pause.

Emily: And it was.

She got a confused look on her face.

Emily: I remember at first hearing that you wouldn't be deployed until August or something.

Me: I don't remember that part. I always remember it being a quick departure, but I wasn't journaling the whole thing yet. What do you remember about the next few months with the family, the church, and the Army once we knew it was going to be a quick ramp-up?

Emily: It took over our lives. That was our only focus. And then things kept changing. The timelines changed and the mission changed. It was a mix of enjoying moments together but trying to figure out what life was going to be like when you were gone.

Deep breath.

Emily: Again, it just took over everything.

I couldn't tell whether this conversation was going to cause more pain, but I wanted to hear from her.

Me: As a mom and wife, did you feel a heightened pressure to do extra stuff so that the kids were okay and so that I would feel supported?

Emily: I don't think it was pressure. We knew that phone call would come someday, and so that's the day it came. It wasn't a surprise but still a shock. I just started preparing for it. That's all I could do.

Me: How did the kids handle the ramp-up?

Emily: I think they did great. It was so hard to explain to them what was happening, especially with how young our kids were then. They didn't understand time, really. You had left on Army trips before, but it was only for two or three weeks at a time, so I didn't know what to say beyond "Daddy is going to be gone for a long time" and things like that.

Me: How do you feel like Saguaro handled it, that crazy month, since I had to leave earlier?

Emily: They handled it wonderfully. I mean, they were shocked for sure, but they really stepped up and handled it by dealing with the logistics and supporting me and you and the kids.

I paused before this next question. I wanted to try to remove my anger from my voice.

Me: What about the Army Reserve and the brigade that was supposed to get us out the door with things like pay and housing?

Her eyes rolled and she sat up straight.

Emily: It was a nightmare. You remember it. Day by day, everything would change. Where would you be? Was there money? It was constant change. It made it difficult for me to figure all of the things that were now on me. I didn't know how our finances were going to work or if they were even going to work. It was so stressful. I just thought we were going to be short financially, but the church stepped up, thankfully, and paid for your vacation time when they didn't have to. From the Army side, it was so hard to get a straight answer.

Me: Do you remember how they kept calling off the mission and telling soldiers to go get their jobs back and then a week later they would tell us that the mission was a go and we needed to quit our jobs again?

Emily: People would put in their notice at work. It was horrible. I remember the conversations you had to have with Gary [Saguaro's moderator]. And of course he was great about it. God, it was awful. Just awful.

Just then, the kids stormed into the room and put on a gymnastics show, which helped alleviate the tension.

Me: How do you remember the final goodbye?

Emily: It was really sad. There were just so many goodbyes. There were all the ones in Phoenix when we got to see you on the weekends. Then there was the one we thought was going to be the final goodbye when you were headed to Fort Hood. It was such a surprise that they decided to unexpectedly give you all a pass before leaving for Kuwait.

I laughed.

Me: I almost didn't take that pass or even tell you about it. Lots of the guys didn't, especially the ones that had deployed before.

Emily: I'm glad you did.

Me: Me too.

She dived back into her memory bank. I could see her eyes searching for and then finding a memory.

Emily: I remember the final weekend being fun. I think the kids thought so too. The day we dropped you off at the airport ... It was so hard ... so, so hard. You were in your uniform. We were all hugging you and crying. I'm sure people around us could probably put the pieces together. All five of us ... This is what it looks like to deploy. People talk about military might, but that airport is what it looks like for all the families left behind.

That was a hard moment, *I thought.*

Me: And then I left. And I was gone for real this time. Did you worry that I was going to die?

With no hesitation:

Emily: Yeah.

Sad and nervous laughter.

Emily: I knew statistically it was unlikely, and I knew at that point you were going to Kuwait, and I knew chaplains did not do the fighting, but it is just so unpredictable. You were still going to a war zone. And remember, we had concerns about your chaplain assistant. At that time, he hadn't passed a physical fitness test or his weapons qualifications. So yeah, I thought about it.

She took a deep breath.

Emily: I was thankful for how much we were able to keep in contact, but every text message and phone call scared me. I thought it was a message saying you had been killed or hurt. Every one of them. I never turned my phone off. I never went places where I knew the service would be bad. I worried about the kids too. I just felt like I always had to be ready and available for the worst.

Me: Did you wonder what life would be like if I died?

Emily: Yeah. I never doubted that we wouldn't okay. It would have changed everything. I guess we would have tried to fill the void as much as possible.

I was uncomfortable.

Me: So, I pushed into Iraq on Friday the thirteenth. Do you remember it?

Emily: Kind of. I just remember it being another change in a long series of changes. I was perfectly happy with you being in Kuwait. I know that you didn't want that. I know you thought that you would be bored and that you wanted a bigger mission, but I didn't want you up in Iraq.

Me: What was it like to parent by yourself carrying all of this?

Emily: It was hard. Overall, I'm proud of how I was able to handle it. I don't think the kids will have too many emotional scars. It was just stressful. Every day. There would be all of these to-do lists that all fell on me. I believe, now, that I probably erred on the side of overplanning and overscheduling so that the kids stayed busy. So that I stayed busy. I just didn't have any backup.

Her response seemed tired still.

Me: At that time, we discussed possibly having you move with the kids to your parents' house in Galveston or even to Kentucky, but we thought it didn't make sense to pull the kids out of their lives here. Do you regret that?

Emily: No. It would have been fun, but it was the right call. Family did a good job of constantly giving us something to look forward to during the whole time. They were good, and we had a great thing with Harper's school.

Me: Was it hard that I missed everything? Birthdays, holidays, and all of that?

Emily: I knew it was probably hardest on you. We still had each other and the special days. We just didn't have you, and so we felt bad for you.

It was hard on me. One of the most regular entries in my journal involved weeping.

Me: I wrote a lot and tried to stay connected. Did that help?

Emily: The kids loved it. They also loved sending you stuff. We had fun going to the store and putting together packages. I tried to imagine what you might like. Eleanor always thought you needed more marshmallows! I think it made them think they were doing something for you. They also loved getting your letters. It was always a big deal. Seeing photos just made them so excited. I would often hold them back until all the letters arrived for each kid and then they would argue over who got theirs read first. Harper and Eleanor even slept with the letters under their pillows frequently.

Me: Do you think the kids liked doing Communion each week?

Emily: I really believe so. I think that's one of their favorite memories and it's probably cemented in them forever. It was a blessing that we got so much contact. It was more than we'd expected and probably helped with the worry.

She was smiling.

Me: Did you feel a pressure to paint a rosy picture for me?

Emily: If I could handle it or if you couldn't do anything about it, I didn't tell you until it was resolved. I only wanted you to be able to keep your focus on things there. That was important to me. I wanted things to be positive. I was just thankful I was able to be in such frequent contact.

Me: Did you think I was keeping things from you in the same way?

Emily: I'm sure you were, but I understood. We knew beforehand that there were lots of things that I wouldn't be able to know. It was hard to explain all of this to people who didn't have a context.

Me: Which reminds me of the FRG (family readiness group), that thing the Army puts together to help the families left behind. Was it helpful?

I felt like I knew how she'd answer this one. I had heard from so many families that they just felt isolated.

Emily: Umm. Kind of. I think Elise was able to do a lot of good stuff, and she tried really hard. With families spread from Tucson to Phoenix and other states, it was challenging, but it was always nice to meet some of the other families since we had that shared connection. It's strange, because for the most part, the other soldiers and their families felt more like characters in our story. Is it different for the active families?

I had heard horror stories about the FRG on the active side too, but it also seemed like they did not realize what a blessing the group could have been for them.

Me: I think so, or at least I would assume so, since they are all located together. The brigade was supposed to put together Yellow Ribbon events to support you. Did those even happen?

Emily: No. Remember, they kept telling us to sign up for events, and then they would email and say that we needed to sign up for a different event. Then it looked like they weren't going to do one, and you intervened, and some of the leadership, and so the brigade put together a support event the weekend before Christmas after y'all had been gone for 90 percent of the deployment and you would be back in a few weeks. The girls had a dance recital so we didn't go.

Me: I forgot that part. Damn.

The memories in my mind started to rumble with frustration. Emily interjected.

Emily: Elise was the only one who made things work. It is just hard to create real relationships throughout the unit in the Reserves.

Me: I know that I still carry a lingering disappointment in that brigade. We've been at war for so long. I just assumed that the send-off, support, and homecoming would be like clockwork. I still cannot believe how much and how often we had to fight our own higher-ups during that deployment. They let so many people down.

Emily: I know.

I switched gears to something I knew would embarrass her.

Me: How did you enjoy celibacy for a year?

Lots of laughter. Too much laughter.

Emily: Enjoy it? No. It was not an ideal situation. It was different for me though. I still had lots of physical contact with the kids. Sam was a baby. They hugged me. They were clingy and they wanted to be held. You were in a situation where people might exchange a handshake and that's it. It was easier on me.

Me: Did you worry that I would be unfaithful?

Emily: Umm. Not really. I trusted you. No. One of the things I love about you is your loyalty. It wasn't a big concern.

I didn't worry either.

Me: How did your faith help you during this time?

Emily: It helped carry me through the randomness of war ... the thoughts of stray bullets and things I couldn't control. I just prayed. In some sense, I used your job to help explain the whole thing to the kids. I told them that you were over there praying for soldiers and so we should pray too.

She thought about it a bit more.

Emily: It was strange, however. As the family of a clergy, we are used to being the ones ministering to others. That year was a beautiful exercise in being ministered to by a community of faith. It felt real. I was always able to call on someone from church. They gave us so much. Sometimes the food lasted for days. I would tell the children that these were acts of love because these people loved them and loved God. I always had someone to call. It was the most helpful thing. They let me know how willing they were to answer the phone. We had people come over to help with a broken water pipe. There were even people who came over to put the girls' bunk beds together as a surprise party. It was just so beautiful.

It felt beautiful hearing her talk like this. So much of the content of the last hour I had never heard before this conversation.

Me: What do you remember about me coming home?

Emily: There was so much excitement and anticipation. I was thrilled that you got through Fort Hood quicker than I thought. We wanted everything perfect. We made signs for a party. I even bought new sheets. When I picked up Harper from school, she was telling her friends. We were so ready.

Me: Are you proud that I went, or do you regret that I went?

Emily: I was proud you went. It was a bonding piece for people within the church who also had spouses deploy over the various wars, kind of like a sisterhood. I am proud. There aren't many people willing to do what you did ... what we did. I am proud that you did it.

I changed the pace.

Me: What was the hardest part of that first year back?

Emily: I think it was the transition back to a partnership. I've always been independent, but I was even more so while you were gone. It was hard having a partner again and being a partner again.

I followed up on that notion of transitions and change. Many parts of our relationship felt different now.

Me: What changed for the better?

Emily: It gave us perspective. The distance created a perspective in which you realize that you can do life without the other person, but then you get the opportunity as you make it through the deployment to intentionally choose to be with each other and our family.

Me: What changed for the worse?

Emily: Anxiety. This experience has effects on people, especially in a combat zone. It has made you more anxious in certain ways and it has done the same to me.

Me: Did it impact the kids?

Emily: The kids are resilient. I don't think it has had a lasting impact on them emotionally. They will all understand it differently as they get older, but I know that they will always be proud that their father served in the Army in Iraq.

It was her most confident answer.

Me: Do you blame Iraq for us not having a fourth kid?

Emily: Yeah.

Long silence. It was clearly still painful. She didn't want to say anything more. I didn't want her to say anything more either. I think that will be one of the great sacrifices we made for our country.

Me: How did the deployment meet and defy your expectations?

Emily: It was hard to know what to expect. In some ways it was easier than I thought it might be. The first month was hard. The kids and I went through an emotional and logistical adjustment. Once we found the new normal, we got in a rhythm. You being gone was part of our daily life, and we talked about you all the time, but we figured out life without. The hardest part was that you were really not there.

Me: How did people surprise you?

Emily: The church surprised me. I've already said that a lot, but it did. I was also surprised at how willing I was to let them help me. It made me uncomfortable sometimes, but I knew I needed the help. My friends surprised me too. Before the deployment, I had friends, but during the deployment they really stepped up and helped with emotional support. I was thankful. They were willing to be my friend even with the demands of these small children.

Me: How did people disappoint you?

She thought about this for a while.

Emily: Umm. I don't think I was disappointed by anyone.

Me: Do you worry that I will deploy again?

Emily: Yes. I figure it will happen at least one more time. It just frustrates me when I watch the news and see politicians being belligerent and inflammatory and I think, "This is it. This is the ramp-up." I mean, you did a great job, and they are going to want you to do it again.

Me: Do you wish that I would resign my commission?

Emily: No.

Me: What was the best piece of advice you got before I left?

Emily: I don't know. I remember you telling me to let people help me so probably that. Most of our friends are our age and haven't gone through this. I just forced myself to let people help me.

I had saved one of the hardest questions for last. These days I felt broken.

Me: One of the things I wrote about in my journals and one of the things that I hoped for the most was that I would come back a better man. In some ways I feel like I did, but I know that in many other ways I didn't. What do you wish that I could make peace with, and what do you wish that I could see that you see within me?

Emily: I don't know if this stems from the deployment, but you came back with a lot of doubts about how good of a husband and father you are. I just wish you could have as much confidence about yourself in those areas as you have in the roles you hold in the Army and the church. I love you.

And I love you too.

Chapter 16

The Historical Disappointment: A Quick Commentary

Early in my teenage years, I remember getting in trouble. To this day I cannot recall what happened, but it probably had something to do with my younger brother. He and I struggled to form a healthy relationship or any of the typical fraternal bonds that were common to others.

Anyway, evidently my parents felt that the punishments they were doling out were no longer an effective deterrent. They were at their wits' end, and so I was taken out to my maternal grandmother's house. Grandma was probably the most important person in my life.

As I sat in front of her, my mom shared with Grandma all the problems I had been creating. I watched with horror as the expression on my grandma's face turned to sadness. She looked at me and said, "Owen, I am so disappointed in you."

I was crushed. I couldn't stop crying. I had failed the biggest source of grace in my life.

Disappointment is a heavy feeling. There is a judgment at its core. True disappointment comes from a place of love and not anger. It is the response one feels and articulates after a line is crossed or a perspective is violated.

It devastated me that I had disappointed my grandma.

I tell this story because that's the feeling that comes to mind when I look back at the United States in 2016 when I was deployed to Iraq. I was disappointed.

As I watched the news that year, I saw a lot of ugliness and civil unrest and a country caving in on itself. I witnessed the rise of white nationalism. I tried to make sense of the shootings of three African-American men—Alton Sterling, Philando Castile, and Keith Lamont Scott—who were shot by police who evidently didn't have to (or at least didn't) follow the same rules of engagement that soldiers in Iraq did. I was moved by the heavy hearts of Native Americans at the Dakota Access Pipeline protests. I mourned the Pulse nightclub shooting and the forty-nine people who lost their lives there.

Worst of all, I watched the most bankrupt presidential election I had ever seen. I listened to the soldiers take sides. The common feeling among the forces was that one candidate represented the worst of our politics while the other candidate represented the worst of our humanity. I listened as one candidate proclaimed, "Grab them by the pussy," as the other candidate tried to explain that her failure to follow the same information protocols that could have ended the career of a commander was not an ethical breach of trust. Both articulated a broken country, and both had an answer. Why did one candidate win? Because the fear embedded in self-preservation is more powerful than an eroded notion of hope.

And we watched this all unfold as we served on the American public's behalf, even though nothing within the news or the political discourse even acknowledged that we were there. Why were we there if no one back home even cared? Was this mission essential to our country's present and future? I prayed for no one to die. How would the honor guard say to the family of the fallen with a sincere face, "on behalf of a grateful country," we present this flag to you?

It hurt. I'm not going to lie. I was disappointed.

Only instead of a sobbing nation trying not to get tears on his grandma's favorite couch, few things within the last few years would suggest that the feelings of people like me even mattered.

Chapter 17

The Aftereffects Part 1

(2018—Tucson, AZ)

Coming home was the hardest part.

Most nights I wake up and I still think that I am there. I still prepare for the walk to the latrine half a football field away. I still pray that my favorite bathroom stall will be clear, clean, and not too warm from use. I still wonder whether there will be other soldiers there in need of counseling. I still dream about my children a half a world away as their little hearts are filled with dreams that I hope they will one day share with me. I am telling you that I wake up most nights and I am genuinely surprised that I am rising from a bed in Tucson. The experience in Iraq was 1/37 of my life, but the thread from that experience still weaves within my everyday life. War created a weird type of grief. I grieved for what I left behind when I went to Iraq. And then I grieved what I left behind in Iraq to come home.

I keep thinking—hoping, really—that it will eventually be difficult emotionally and spiritually to drift back to Iraq, but it isn't. I still think that at any moment I will be back. And part of me finds comfort in that nightmare, and part of me longs for it even though I dare not articulate that in front of family, especially my wife and children.

After one year, I firmly believe in this truth: Iraq didn't create any cracks in my personhood or relationships, but it sure did find the cracks that were already there—even the ones I barely noticed or was unaware existed—and it made them more pronounced and unavoidable. I wonder if David felt the same during all of his experiences of war. The psalms proclaim,

A thousand may fall at your side,
ten thousand at your right hand,
but it will not come near you;
For you will only observe with your eyes.

David knew. You can come back but you are different. Forever. One year removed and I was starting to see that more and more.

It is not an easy story, however. There is so much that is miserable about deploying to a combat zone. I've spent much of this book wallowing in that story. The experience was incredible, however, and I pray that fact is palpable to you. Over the holidays this last year, I made the mistake of telling a friend that I would go back if I was tasked to do so. The look on his face was a mix of sheer disbelief, anger, and pain. I had hurt his feelings. He had encouraged me, prayed for me, sent treats through the mail, and helped my family at home. That I would go back willingly was a slap in the face. I wondered whether he would still be as helpful if I deployed again. I don't know.

Deployment, especially to a combat theater, is one of the most unique experiences in existence. Do you know what it's like to turn on CNN, see all of the world's attention turned to an event that is more than a battle for the liberation of a province or people, but a very battle against one of the purest manifestations of evil in our lifetime, and to realize that you are there, that the work you complete each day directly impacts the effort that you see on that screen? I do. It was one of the most meaningful experiences a person can live. I lived it. I loved it.

And then I went home to a country completely at odds with itself, but that complexity had nothing to do with the wars still being waged on their behalf.

It is strange. If the military is referenced within daily discourse, the conversation is detached from the humanity of the soldiers. We are reduced to objects, tools, and bludgeons, and we are wielded by our elected leaders as if we were characters in a video game. There are disabling consequences to the psyche of a people when war becomes something that always happens elsewhere in distant places with people who don't look or talk like us. As a country, we are too ready to engage in combat. We are too ready to support it and not consider the consequences on generations of distant communities. When war is something that we can wage on others, perpetually, while not giving a second thought to it as we drive to the store, we are in trouble. Additionally, long-term damage comes from multiple deployments for soldiers who fall through the cracks of communities around the country.

I get my share of gratitude from friends and neighbors, especially when in my uniform. I appreciate it. It makes me stand taller. I see the pride in the faces of my family since they intimately shared in this sacrifice too. What I don't understand, and what I wish for, is a more engaged public wrestling with the reality of all these years of war. I want an honest discussion on the moral injury of our country—the bloodlust, the rise of toxic masculinity, the hollowing out of our souls and our forces, the hubris that leads us to believe we can wage indefinite wars with contractors, foreign forces, and logistics without any consequence to our people. I am thankful for the sacrifices I made, but I would like those sacrifices to shape the future of the nation I served in a way that reflects the honor I and so many others put into our duty.

Luckily, I guess, there is still time. Iraq and Afghanistan are unchanged. North Korea seems to be an emerging reality. One month ago, I swore in a soldier who was an infant when those planes hit the twin towers in New York City. I still remember standing outside President Bush's Texas retreat and protesting the Iraq War in 2006. Let that sink in for a minute! I used to think that my generational cohort, Gen X, was going to be distinctive in being the one generation that conducted our nation's longest wars, but it is looking as if that will be a shared distinction with the Millennials. Damn. There is a real chance that my children will one day be called to serve in wars in places from which we swore we would protect them.

So, I would go back. At least that's what I say to myself. But then I look at my family. And then I know I shouldn't. Over the last year I have been surprised by the number of soldiers whose relationships have ended in divorce.

Iraq was hard on us as a family. It took a while to see the depth of it. I still remember the glow and the feeling of reunion when I first came back home. I found this old text thread from a few weeks after coming home:

"How's your family? Seems like they made it through it, right?" My old college friend messaged me through Facebook right after I got back.

Silence on my end.

"I didn't even know you were gone, since you didn't post anything about it on social media," he wrote.

"Yep. Since Emily and the kids were going to be home by themselves, we didn't want to draw a lot of attention to the fact that I was gone," I wrote back.

"Are the kids excited that you are back?"

"I think so. Harper and Elle won't let me out of their sight. I think that they are afraid that if I leave I'll vanish back to Iraq. Sam is still trying to figure all of this out. He wasn't even a year old when all of this started."

I paused.

"It is hard. I see the distance in his face. I think he was beginning to think that I was just a video on the iPad like some other show he watches. From time to time, he calls me 'Pastor Owen' like his friends do at daycare," I texted back.

"What about Emily?"

"She was a champ. I don't know how she did it all," I replied, and ended, "I guess it might take some time to unpack all of this, but I feel like I am living a blessing."

It did.

Iraq scarred us. We are different. I am different. Sometimes the things that fall apart, as the psalmist sung, aren't always the result of war, but all the things that didn't happen because of the deployment. As they fall, they become like salt in all the cracks you didn't even know were there.

I still feel that every moment is pregnant with the possibility that I will be asked to hop a C-130 back to Iraq. Even now, I can still feel the adrenaline of Iraq. I can smell it seeping through my pores. I can still feel the power of the need as I helped soldiers work through some of the most difficult seasons of their lives. None of it is healthy, I know. As a result, I struggle with being fully present to myself, to my family, to my vocation. I also struggle with the fear that people wish I were still deployed. It is no secret: I am a difficult person to live with and work alongside. I very rarely turn off, and I expect of others the same that I expect of myself, which is admittedly intense. Buried within the romanticism of a loved one at war is the reality that life can be easier when that person is gone.

I worry about this with my family. I torment myself with a nightmare: that they need me to be gone too. That it was easier when I was in Iraq because there was a common enemy—time—that rooted and bonded them together. I interpret this in different ways within my family. For the children, every day was like a holiday as they got to go and do all sorts of special things. Grandparents sent endless packages in the mail filled with toys and goodies. At first when I came back, this season of indulgence was even bigger, but now they don't receive the deployment benefit as much. We still have fun, but things aren't as centered on their entertainment now. I sense it differently with Emily. I feel as if Emily has been reluctant to deviate from her deployment routine. I don't believe her reluctance is centered in an animosity toward me from my return, but more like a motherly or self-defense mechanism, as if she too believes that I could be gone at a moment's notice. In that way, I now often feel like an outsider to my family. I am like a visitor to their lives, no longer an integrated part of it. They enjoy their time with me, and we have many good moments, but I recognize how the demands of my profession and the lingering effects of the deployment have complicated their lives. I am like the extended visit from a distant loved one whose time is a mixed blessing.

I feel as if my inability to be present is a slap in the face to my family. I see the sting, but I still turn my attention toward the Middle East several times a day. So, I go to bed every night and I pray for two things: first, that when I wake up I will be closer to coming home completely; and second, that the sacrifices my family and I made will not only bring us together more intentionally but that we will also help shape a future worthy of those sacrifices.

Coming home is the hardest part.

Chapter 18

The Aftereffects Part 2

(2019—Tucson, AZ)

I sat in the parking lot. The car engine was still running. Maybe two hundred yards in front of me was the entrance to the VA. It was easy to see since there were so few vehicles crowding my view so early in the morning. I brought the last of the warm coffee up to my mouth. It was strong. I was not.

I tried to take in a deep breath, but I couldn't. My lungs felt like they were drowning. I couldn't catch my breath. My prickly skin crawled, and my ears were sensitive to most noises above a whisper. I was a hot mess.

In my soul, I could hear the declarative words of Jesus: "The spirit is willing, but the flesh is weak." I wouldn't say that these words stung, but they were painfully descriptive. I was broken. I still believed in prayer, but I had started to lose faith.

No one knew I was there. Absolutely no one. It felt like a complete failure to be there. I had yet to figure out a way to tell my family or really anyone in my life about my decision to seek help. I was at a loss as to how or whether to disclose it to the church, even as I was helping Saguaro shape a mental health ministry.

So, I didn't tell a soul. I was broken. I was alone. I was literally suffocating in anxiety. I didn't know how to give myself the same grace that I shared with others on a daily basis.

I have often remarked that we lead lives woven in irony and grace, and this could not have been a more accurate statement of where I was exactly two years after Iraq.

On the surface, one could have claimed that I was leading a charmed existence. I had received an early promotion to major, a highly selective honor. Our family was thriving, funny, and photo-genic. The church was living into its future and finally building the community kitchen that had eluded them for over twenty years. I was even recognized as one of Tucson's 40 Under 40.

But I didn't feel it. Why was coming home still so hard?

And so, I shut off the engine and walked into a door I prayed led to peace.

And all the while, with each step toward that entrance, I plead-ed for God's help, for "the spirit is willing, but the flesh is weak."

Chapter 19

The Healing

(2020—Tucson, AZ)

God of mercy and hope,
I am grateful. I am humbled. I am breathing.

I am grateful for the VA.
I am grateful for the counselor that helped me heal.
I am grateful that I was given a path back to who I am.

I am humbled that you still call me to serve.
I am humbled that my heart can still create avenues for people to experience your grace.
I am humbled that your steadfast love never gave up on me.

I am breathing and laughing.
I am breathing and dreaming.
I am breathing and living into a future created by you.

I confess that I know my story needs to look more balanced and present, but I know my story doesn't end in Iraq.

I don't know if you ever completely get to come home, so hear my prayer from the deserts of the American Southwest and from the rivers in Babylon.

In the name of the one that walked beside me, Jesus Christ,

Amen.

* * *

(Or so I thought.)

Epilogue

The New Road

(2021—Fort Stewart, GA)

I grew up in Western Kentucky along the banks of the mighty Ohio River. Imagine endless cornfields and small town charm. Before you romanticize it too much, imagine it drowning in humidity. Though our town was picturesque, it was sparse commercially. We had a Walmart and its kissin' cousin, Rural King. That was about it.

Frequently, the need would arise for one thing or another that our hometown didn't have. We'd make the run over to Indiana for shopping trips or to visit the fancy eating establishments. To get to Indiana, we had to cross over the twin bridges, which were amazing feats of engineering. These enormous and surprisingly long iron structures were perpetually being repaired.

As we traveled the bridge, we often played a silly game: Hold your breath for the duration of the trip over the bridge, and you'd have a wish granted. These twin bridges were lengthy—a half mile, my memory seems to suggest. We kids would encourage whoever was driving to go as fast as possible. I remember one of my friends' dads thinking it was funny to slow down during these games and watch our faces turned purple.

One Sunday on our way to the Red Lobster, I tried to convince my grandpa to play this slow-down prank on my cousins in the back seat. He laughed. "Golly Moses, boy, no one can stay on a bridge forever. We got to keep driving. You just better wish the bridge holds!"

I have thought a lot about bridges over the last four years. When I started this book, I reckoned that my calling in ministry was to be a builder of bridges, maybe one as marvelous as the twin bridges of my childhood. I figured this twin bridge would fashion roads between the military and civilian worlds and between the wearers of those black hats and the churches seeking to offer healing to the soldiers' souls. I hoped that this book's stories would foster relationships and insights between these communities.

As I retold those stories while writing this book, I often found myself holding my breath as I crossed over between differing banks of reality. I don't know whether I was holding on to the hope of a wish granted (that you, the reader, would actually find meaning in this book) or just that the bridge I was building would hold.

And then 2020 happened.

As we all lived, COVID ravaged families and shut down entire communities. Churches became virtual and creative. Racial injustice refused to be placated with platitudes and promises of thoughts and prayers. Conspiracy theories radicalized large segments of the public. Sexual assault and harassment were malignant cancers within military posts. A mental health crisis emerged, and the military saw pronounced increases in suicides. The 2020 presidential election was worse than that of 2016, and the military was frequently placed in uncomfortable positions as it sought to maintain its apolitical posture. The year ended with a failed armed insurrection of the nation's capitol during the certification of the Electoral College. That year was something else. I don't imagine that anyone ended the year unscathed.

I wrote previously within these pages that though a deployment doesn't necessarily create cracks within an individual or community, it definitely finds and exacerbates them. Millions of households in America were learning this lesson in a very real way. Like the experience I underwent in Iraq, 2020 brought out the best in some people, but it also broke way too many.

It should be no surprise, then, that my ministerial call changed. Like my grandpa had said, I couldn't stay on the bridge forever.

During 2020, I experienced increased demands at the church as we recreated it virtually every few weeks. The Army Reserve was stuck in a holding pattern, which made it almost impossible to minister to soldiers that I now never saw and who were spread out over the continental United States and Hawaii. Every time I opened my Army email there were potential plans of mobilizations, deployments, or special assignments. The new hunger nonprofit I had founded was rising to meet the challenges of our neighbors, but that meant considerable amounts of grant writing and development. Much to the chagrin of my kids, I became their distance learning teacher. It was ... umm ... a lot. I felt as rickety as those old twin bridges perpetually under repair. It definitely didn't feel like a silly game.

Against this backdrop, a new set of orders emerged within the chaos. Literally. Through a rare exception to standard policy, I was transferred into the Regular Army. This transfer will be accompanied by another deployment to the Middle East during the summer of 2021. I will be relocating our family to Fort Stewart, Georgia. Of all the scenarios being created by the needs of the Army due to the cracks of 2020, it was my wish to senior leadership and the Chaplain Corps that the Army would consider a proactive approach to my service. Ideally, it would be nice to have whatever suited the needs of the Army undergirded with some type of stability. I got my wish, I guess. Receiving those orders was a moment of pride, bewilderment, and hope.

So, the week before Thanksgiving, almost five years to the day of announcing the pending deployment to Iraq, I resigned as senior minister of Saguaro Christian Church. My beloved Saguaro. As in 2016, the church rose to the occasion to offer love and support. For that, and for everything, I love them so much.

It is a weird phenomenon to leave a place you love in order to serve another calling of love. It was also a strange feeling to realize how much of my identity was tethered to congregational ministry as I packed up the boxes within my office. I can't help but laugh. When I was exiting seminary, I figured that I would serve a church for maybe a year. I wondered whether God would realize God's mistake in letting me preach and direct me to a more suitable path. That was fourteen years ago. With each transition moment, I simply asked: What does faithfulness look like in this season of ministry? The answer became the road I took, and for fourteen years that road went back and forth on a twin bridge of faith.

But now it was time to keep driving.

* * *

As my family pulled into the front gate of Fort Stewart, the humidity welcomed us first. It felt a bit like an old, familiar home nestled on the banks of another river in the South. I waited my turn in the row of cars. Behind me were our children's small faces pressed to the windows as their minds raced with sadness and excitement at the future. I kept my eyes in front of me and thought about this book. I thought about the bridge I sought to construct. I inched closer to the guard at the gate, and I exhaled. I thought about my grandfather. I think he'd be proud of me. I remember his words: "Just hope the bridge holds."

Acknowledgments

This book is a faith-centered celebration of family, friendship, and community done right.

To begin, I cannot thank enough my parents Judy and Rick Chandler, my in-laws Mike and Joan Rigsby, and my brother-in-law Dustin Rigsby. I never worried about my wife and children being forgotten because you all went above and beyond to wrap them with love ... and so many presents.

I am grateful to Chief Dave Slaven. You were a great friend, an amazing barbecue master, and the steadiest leader I've ever met.

I am grateful for the command team of the 336 CSSB. You led with honor. You brought us home.

I will never forget my beloved Saguaro Christian Church. You stood by me. You prayed for me. You wrote me letters, which I kept. You cared for my family. You cared for our soldiers. You didn't fire me! You are the best of what is possible in church.

I am grateful for the steadfast correspondence from my Aunts Pat and Sandy, and from Thom Gibson and Shirley Estes, who also provided me a space in which to write this book. I am especially mindful of the letters of Kerry Swindle. She graciously let me process some of the spiritual and existential dilemmas that the deployment created for me. Many of those letters helped form these chapters. It was poetic, then, that her husband, Tim Swindle, helped me polish the early draft of this book. Kerry and Tim are forever in my heart.

I am grateful for the ways that simple moments and searching conversations can change the trajectory of your life. So, thanks for the beer, Cameron Gibson; the elevator ride filled with wisdom, Steve Doan; and thank you, Russ Boyd, for your response to one of my meandering monologues on the military: "You know the Army has chaplains, right?"

I am grateful to Suzzane Perkins. You helped bring me back when I walked through those doors at the VA. God bless your counsel, wisdom, and accountability.

Last and probably most importantly, I want to thank the God of my calling. There have been so many times that I've had to wonder whether God has buyer's remorse about using someone like me for the benefit of the gospel. I know that all too often my calling looks like the classic lyric from the hymn "Come Thou Fount of Every Blessing":

> Prone to wander, Lord, I feel it,
> Prone to leave the God I love;
>
> And so ...
>
> Here's my heart, O take and seal it,
> Seal it for Thy courts above.

Fort Stewart, GA

January 15, 2021

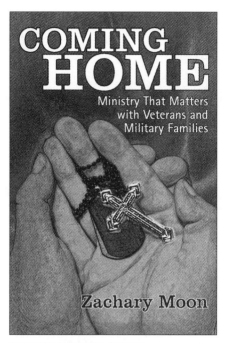